# THE ACCIDENTAL ADVENTURER

## By Nahla Summers

The events and conversations in this book have been set down to the best of the author's ability, although some names and details have been changed. We can guarantee that all events described actually happened, though on occasion the author has taken a rough summary of what was said in conversations, because quite frankly, it is set over 10 years, no one's memory is that good!

ISBN 978-1-7398354-4-6

To follow more adventures go to
www.nahlasummers.com

This is dedicated to you, the reader of this book.
I hope when you finish it, you will understand why.

# Table of Contents

# Chapter 1

## The beginning

*"There are moments when I wish I could roll back the clock and take all the sadness away, but I have the feeling that if I did, the joy would be gone as well."*
—*Nicholas Sparks, A Walk to Remember*

I woke to my heart beating so fast I thought I would lose my breath forever. Eyes wide and breath rasping, I was overwhelmed by a feeling of impending doom. Maybe I would fail? Was I just not good enough, after all this time and all this work? It was a feeling I dreaded, and it haunted me as I navigated the biggest challenge I had undertaken to date.

Eventually I sat up in bed, swung round and put my feet on the familiar brown carpet of my parents' spare room. Everything I had ever owned was up for sale and suddenly I wondered if it was all worth it. Would I ever make a difference?

Eighteen months of planning, and everything that could have gone wrong did. I constantly questioned if it was a sign that I should stop. The past eight years of challenges had made me fearless. Fast paced juggernauts flying past me and near misses were never far from my memories. Would this be the challenge that would finally see me fail? Would I lose a limb, or injure myself so badly that I could never do another challenge? The future felt so uncertain.

I reached across to the clothes hanging over the chair, pulling on a pair of sports leggings and a training top. I walked down the stairs, the summer sun only just peeking through the curtains. The light caught in the gaps and my breath caught with it.

I walked into the small, compact, perfectly organised kitchen; my mother's love evident in every part of it. I made my usual breakfast: quinoa, hot raspberries, live yoghurt and cacao nibs. I sat down and sighed as I followed the ritual of mindful eating. I knew diet could be the make or break of this challenge... I'd learnt this lesson the hard way two years ago, while travelling across America.

Sinking into the comfort of an armchair that was older than me, I felt a sense of security and homeliness. The sun was rising, and through the window, it caught the picture frame of a younger me. A smell of flowers wafted in from my mothers' abundant garden as I opened my laptop for an early morning video call with the sponsor of my next challenge.

This simple and easy life seemed at odds with the corporations I often work with. As the faces arrived on the screen in front of me, their expressions told me so much and yet so little. I felt the unease rise in me, but I smiled and greeted everyone with my usual external optimism.

"Hi, how are you?"

Everyone on the screen smiled back and joined the chorus of greetings.

Then, the main sponsor cut to the chase. "So, how are things going?"

"Oh yes, it's all going well," I said, with a smile. "We've obviously moved from the challenge happening in Europe as I mentioned in my last email. But I think the UK will give some great coverage and, while it wasn't the plan, I think writing

KINDNESS across England will give some incredible opportunities–"

The sponsor responded without even blinking. "I don't think it will be possible for us to sponsor you now."

No one else reacted. I could feel their eyes on my face, waiting for my reaction, watching to see what I would do or say next. I took a moment to steady my breath.
"Ah, ok."
More conversation followed, but I had stopped listening, their words becoming white noise as I started to think of what to do next. A wave of electricity coursed through my body and the hairs on the backs of my arms stood on end.

Outwardly, I smiled and took the crushing news as gracefully as I could. There were too many people on the call for me to question the decision without appearing desperate. With just a matter of weeks to go and continued knockbacks, my confidence and self-worth had been getting lower and lower. Now, I was watching it pack its bags and walk out of the door without so much as a backward glance.

Hearing that they were unable to provide the financial support that they had promised had a physical effect on my gut. I felt the visceral kick that started the familiar sinking spiral. My stomach was turning and churning. All of the problems I thought I had solved came rushing back into my mind, casting a heavy fog over the path I'd set out for myself.

I shut my laptop and glanced up at the picture of my younger self. How did I get here? Why was this happening to me, just two weeks to go until my next challenge? Why now, when I needed support more than ever?

For the first time in months, I let the emotion pour out of me, loudly and unapologetically and wholeheartedly. Tears that I'd stubbornly held back finally made their presence known, spilling down my face. Everything felt in jeopardy. Everything, including my own sanity, was on the line.

Later that day, my dreams of gaining a support vehicle and a driver also became a distant memory. I now didn't know how I would actually achieve the 5,000 miles I needed to seal the world record, but giving up was not an option. This perseverance didn't come naturally to me. When I was younger, it had been so easy for me to walk away when tough challenges presented themselves but, when I met Paul, he changed all that.

Falling in love with Paul has been a highlight of my life. Paul was six foot something with a full head of dark hair that, with time, became peppered with grey. He had no defining features, no big nose or small lips, although sometimes I poked fun at his ears. He should have been instantly attractive, but I didn't see it straight away. We'd been friends a long time before something changed. In the end, Paul and I fell in love with the people that we both were on the inside, which is comforting and heart-breaking in equal measure.

Whenever Paul was chatting to someone and I sidled up into the crook of his arm to join in, it was like coming home. I had always belonged in the warmth of that place. He told me I lit up a room, but I now know that I was shining for him. What I know for sure, even a decade since his unexpected death, is that we were intrinsically linked, as though he took over a part of my very being. I knew what he was going to say and what he was thinking. For the first time in my 32 years of existence, I was myself.

He was as some might describe, 'a bit of a one', and was not always known for making the best decisions in his personal life. However, he was funny and, despite his claims and personal history, surprisingly loyal. His life had routine and structure, making him predictable in some ways, but he was very spontaneous when it came to other parts of who he was.

Paul, unlike me, was a pretty practical person. He was a fixer of all things and it was another reason why I loved him so much. When the car broke down it was fixed with the help of a coat hanger. When I had troubles, he managed to fix those too. He always found a solution to everything. On all the adventures I'd been on since his death, I wish he had been with me... But if he were there, I would never have become the person I am today.

We had many things going for us, and laughter was one of them. With a quick jovial wit that kept us going through the everyday challenges we faced and overcame together; he'd do hilarious things to make me laugh. He showed me it was ok to argue and then move on together. I showed him that it was ok to be accepted for who you were. He would make my breakfast every morning and surprise me by doing wonderful things in the house. I felt safe. Nine years on I still sometimes find myself wishing him back.

So often, it is moments of mundane mumblings that shine from my memories the most. Lying in his arms, the four white walls surrounding us in our pine framed bed. It was the time of day with him I loved the most. Just us.

"I'm not sure I could ever live without you," he said. "If something happened to you, I couldn't go on." I felt the pressure of his arms encompass me. It was as if he knew something bad was on the horizon, he just couldn't place it. "You are never going to be without me," I said, trying to lighten the moment. "Just don't stuff it up."

One of the many things Paul and I did together was write a joint bucket list. I'll be honest, I made him. "What do you want to do together? I mean, what have you always dreamt of doing?" I asked him in curiosity one evening. "I don't know," he said. "There's no point in doing a list. I'll never have the money to do these things."

Even then, those words were what I needed to drive us forwards into the unknown. We needed a plan. I loved him, and we were making this plan together.

"Well, we won't know until we write them down," I said, rummaging around for a pen and a scrap of paper. He smiled and picked up the pen.

Planning for the future had always been my safe place: make a list, book to see a show, plan to visit a friend. It was what got me to the age of 32 still holding onto my sanity by the skin of my teeth. After university I had fallen into a career of leadership which paid well. I was driven and focused, but I made lots of mistakes along the way. I learnt little from them at first and was stuck in 10-hour days which consumed my working week. I made rash judgements, got offended quickly and understood little about my emotional self. I spent most of my time wrapped up in my own story: internalising my life, the people I met and the situations I found myself in. I spent considerable time with my thoughts in the past and then, to relieve myself of that pain, I would jump to the future, running towards whatever was next. Unable to be in the present, capitalism ruled my life. Get the money, save some, spend some. Repeat. It felt comfortable.

Planning came naturally to me, but not to Paul. It took him two weeks to write his bucket list. I copied the list out neatly and pinned it in plain sight on our notice board; a physical reminder of the life we wanted to create.

After he died, the bucket list tore into my very being, taunting me. It reminded me of the fictitious limb I had lost and the broken heart I was left with. In the end, the list was the thing that saved me. It gave me a focus. I would grow alone with those dreams, but I would make them a reality in his name. I was glad he hadn't had to suffer the pain of grief that he feared so much. As I look back, maybe that's what love truly is: taking someone's pain so they don't have to endure it.

My time with Paul taught me that love is not made up of all the things you do with someone, it's simply being in their presence and feeling overwhelmed by what lies between you. You know, I think if that type of love came along now, I may hold on to it a little tighter than I did. His death showed me that I hadn't looked hard enough at what we had, savouring the seconds and not sweating the small stuff.

Our final conversations and messages swirl around in my memories as if somehow, we both knew what was around the corner. In truth, we had no idea. Three days before his death we walked out onto the beach and he complained because his arm hurt, a sign of something more serious happening with his heart. The night before he died, he was sat in his usual place at the table. I was crouched over my laptop on the sofa, multitasking between chatting and finishing some final tasks for work the next day. We'd somehow got onto a conversation about life and regrets.

"If my life was to end tomorrow, I would feel I had done enough," I said, still engrossed in my laptop. "My friend and I use to talk about that years ago, but I feel that now more than ever. I've never said no to an opportunity and feel I've lived life fully."

There was a silence, not a big one, almost too tiny for anyone else to notice.

I looked up and as I did, he said, "Well, that's a depressing thought." His face contoured into a half smile, half grimace.

The irony now is not lost on me. Not only for the most obvious reason – that Paul would lose his life – but because the years since his death have seen me give more to the world than I ever could have hoped.

The day I dropped him off for the fateful charity cycle ride, I sent him a text to tell him I loved him. I was so compelled to send the message that I pulled to a stop on the main road, hazard lights flashing. A few hours later, his name flashed up on my phone. Sat at the desk in my open plan office I moved over to answer it, look out of the window and gain some privacy. "How you doing, babes?", "I'm not feeling great. I feel like I'm having a heart attack, I might call an ambulance." He responded calmly. "Ah ok, where are you?" I responded, mimicking his calmness. "I'll call you back in 10 minutes babes." he said. I had no reason to believe he wouldn't, but it would be the last conversation he would have. He died on the side of the road where he stood. For the entire day as people came and went from the hospital, I felt the biggest wave of love for him – more than I thought was possible. It was as if he had passed all his love over to me.

The days that followed were full of shock and grief. No-one brought food or flowers, few people came and went. That had not been our life. It had just been us, a bubble we had formed that was safe and familiar. Now I understood how fragile bubbles could be. I ranted and talked in riddles, barely holding it together while I tried to function in society. The funeral came and went, and I was alone in our house with a future that could never be realised, pinned as a list to the noticeboard.

I spent the first month in a state of shock, asking no one in particular, "Where have you gone?"

I didn't know where he was, but I wanted to be there with him, even if it was a horrible, dark place. It had to be better than being without him. So, I lived with the ghost of him. It was the safest place for me to exist. I didn't want to leave the house as that was where I felt his presence the most, where there was something left of him.

I crawled to the doctors one day when it all got too much. They told me they could give me some tablets. I knew that no tablet would solve this heart-breaking sadness. No drug could or should fix that. Grief is all-encompassing. It seeps into your bones and becomes a solid functioning state of who you are. I didn't try to numb myself or hide from the sadness, I let it wash over me. I drowned so many times, but what I learnt is there is power in letting your emotions take whatever form they need to.

As the weeks and months progressed, I realised I hadn't understood my reality well enough. For so long I had talked about making a change in my life, creating a life out of the corporate world, one with purpose and meaning. I had somehow falsely convinced myself that the promise of the life I could live meant I was making a difference in the world.

Paul and I had a house on the beach, and when the sun set, the colours would fill the front bedroom, a kaleidoscope of colour. In usual circumstances it would provide great peace and joy. But after Paul's death, the beach and the beautiful sunsets were just an unbearable reminder of all that was no more. On one particular day, I decided to step out onto the beach as the sun set. I crossed the long straight road up over the grass bank and onto the concrete walkway. I passed the bench where we used to sit and headed up the short incline over the dunes. As I reached the top of the slope, I could see a horse being ridden in figures of eight on the sand.

The orange sunset sparkled on the distant sea. Watching the horse mesmerised me. There were no thoughts about what my life had become and what I had lost. The sand was damp and compact, so I crouched down and sat on my heels. My jogging pants hung off me with the weight I had lost, the bottoms of the legs trailing in the wet sand.

I noticed a man walking his dog along the beach, taking slow, steady steps. I went back to watching the horse's tricks. Suddenly, the man with the dog was beside me. I remember he had grey hair, but if you put him in a line-up today, I'm not convinced I could point him out. I stood up out of politeness, tightening the string around my jogging pants.

"Is the horse yours?" he asked.

"Oh, no, it's not mine," I responded.

With no mental strength to provide any more dialogue than that. He didn't take offence. Instead, he immediately compensated with his own stories.

"Ah, wonderful isn't it? Horses are so incredible. I've not seen anyone do this in this country before. I saw it a lot in America. I worked out there for many years and saw the impact that horses can have. There were a number of stables around me that had been set up to support people who had a physical or mental disability. The horses appeared to have huge healing powers." I didn't say anything.

"People who had not been able to communicate seemed to somehow find a way to communicate through and with, the horses. There is so much we don't understand about the world."

I looked at the horse and so did he. He continued to share stories of his time in America and his life. There was a rhythm to his voice that gave me comfort. I didn't speak much, only to confirm or agree.

After 10 minutes or so, his phone rang and he took the call, leaving me with my thoughts. In many ways, there was nothing significant about this encounter. But for me, in my place of deep depression, it was as if he had taken me outside of my own inner story of sadness and, for a moment, stopped me drowning in my grief. At the time, my unhappiness seeped from my very being. He saw that, never asking what was wrong or trying to fix me. He just talked about a story of positivity.

Watching him walk back along the beach, I felt something inside me shift. The change was so profound that some nine years later, I can still feel precisely what I felt back then. Before speaking to the man, my peripheral vision had been complete darkness. There was no future. Now I felt I was looking down a long tunnel with a glimmer of light at the end. Through his kindness, hope had arrived in my life, and hope is all we can wish for in our darkest moments. As I walked back to the house, I knew that this moment was pivotal. I didn't know how exactly; I just knew that it was.

There are not many moments you remember for so long, especially such a simple one. But that sandy walk is imprinted in my memory. My thoughts, my mind, my newfound hope. As time went on over the coming months, it was the kindness of people that became more and more important. Kindness was saving my life.

Paul is gone. Even his memory has become a memory in itself. This social movement to spread the message of kindness started because of Paul, but it has become so much bigger than him and certainly bigger than me. The message of kindness is more important than either of us or our love.

My life can never go back to what it was. It's as if the vessel has melted and changed shape in the sun, and it won't fit back into the form it was before. The bubble we had been living in had burst, and we all know that bubbles cannot be put back together.

There was no way for me to have known that I would travel the world, cycling thousands of miles and overcoming so many challenges by relying on the power of kindness. But here I am, sharing the truth that when your world falls apart around you and you feel you will never be good enough, you can rise from the ashes and build a truly astounding life.

How I got there, well, that is a story in itself.

# Chapter 2

## ElliptiGO World Record challenge: 2020

## "Plan early, plan twice"

Every year since Paul's death, I have completed an annual challenge to promote kindness. When I finished my 500-mile walk in April 2019, I immediately started organising the 2020 challenge.

As I sat on the edge of a low wall above Sandbanks beach in the south of England, my eyes drawn back up to the never-ending horizon of blue ripples, I realised that after 12 months of planning it felt like I'd done nothing at all. The sea was a place for me to contemplate life and I was haunted by Paul's familiar voice in the breeze saying, 'plan early, plan twice'.

The original idea was to complete 20 kindness challenges in 20 different countries. I'd set off from England in June 2020 and spend the next three months travelling through Europe, ticking off countries along the way. The idea for this challenge, like all of them, developed from the suggestions of many people. I like to talk to people and I love even more to listen. It is always a great honour to be brought into someone else's story, so I listen intently when people make suggestions for the challenges I might try. People are able to live their dreams through me and there is something beautiful about that. This particular challenge, though, had evolved into the ridiculous and I had no idea if it was possible. It was a series of unknown elements with no handbook to follow.

My aim was to attempt a World Record on an ElliptiGO, a bike without a seat, travelling approximately 4,800 miles while completing kindness activities along the way. Free Listening in Latvia, picking up litter in Belarus, feeding 100 people in Romania. You get the idea. Each act of kindness had its own logistical challenges: I needed to organise a support vehicle, find places to stay, pay drivers, make sure I fuelled my body correctly, find videographers, attract sponsors and get legal approval. And, I would need to document everything for the World Record. The challenge just kept expanding and every time I spoke to someone it grew a little more. Eventually, I had to stop saying yes. If I wasn't careful, I'd be off to Mars before the year was out.

2020, the year of hope, started well. The day the ElliptiGO arrived by courier it was a surprisingly mild day in early January and the sun was shining. If you didn't know better, you could have mistaken the British wintertime for a balmy spring day. The bare trees swaying in the breeze were the only hint of the season.

This unusual contraption was totally new to me and there was something both nerve-wracking and exciting about that. As I looked at the box, I felt a wave of something barely recognisable to me these days. Fear.

I pulled the long, large, coffin-like box into the front room of my childhood home. The cardboard was thick and robust and totally out of place in my mother's 'Home and Country' artistic decor. There, between the lovingly restored armchairs and perfectly positioned paintings, was the fireplace where I toasted marshmallows in my youth. Against that, the jarring sight of this new, unusual, bright red contraption which I had never ridden but had committed to attempt a World Record on. As I yanked the ElliptiGO out of the box, the difference in my life from then to now was striking.

My youth for the most part was quiet and uneventful. I would bounce a ball against the house to pass the time and sit in the living room hugging my grandparents who visited regularly. I would walk, swim, and make pancakes on Sundays with my father. I would hide behind my mother when someone came to our door, curious about life but scared of what might face me. My mother described me as a child who needed reassurance and lacked bravery. Today, back in the same space I grew up in, I could feel the disparity between the child I once was and the person I was now.

The ElliptiGO was surprisingly easy to put together. It looks similar to a cross trainer you might find in the gym but with a couple of wheels to get it moving. It arrived with just a set of handlebars to be popped into the frame.

Once put together, I wheeled the contraption out of the front door and into the sunshine. The smell of the sweet, exposed earth of winter hit me. In front of the house there is a small incline in the road that leads to the middle of the town. I jumped on the ElliptiGO. It was too hard to push down on the pedals and I was not familiar with the gearing. I tried to do all the actions required to keep going up the hill, but I panicked and ultimately the stand-up bike came to a halt and subsequently so did I. The bike fell sideways, thumping the ground with a slow and painful thud. My legs were tangled in the frame, lying slap bang in the middle of the road while my mother filmed it for prosperity from the front door. A large bruise started to bloom across my thigh. What had at first been a fleeting sense of fear was now an overwhelming sense of anxiety. I was about to travel 5,000 miles on this bike that I couldn't even pedal up the road. As I hobbled back to the front door, bike in hand, I looked at my mother's panicked face, and smiled reassuringly.

"I'll get used to it soon enough, it's all fine." I didn't know if it was true but saying anything else seemed futile.

Later that day I asked a friend to come over and we walked to the local town's car park with the ElliptiGO. I needed to feed off her confidence and told her as much. We chose a car park on a hill with a small roundabout at the bottom. This was incidentally the same hill my father watched me learn to ride my bike. He taught me to scoot my feet along the ground to propel the bike along. Eventually, after a few weeks, having got my balance I lifted my feet up to roars of joy from my father as he ran to get my mother. The memory of that day, some 30 years later, had never been clearer.

This day, it was quiet, with only a few parked cars. My friend jumped on the ElliptiGO as though she had ridden it a thousand times before. I tried not to compare or feel uneasy. Instead, I simply allowed her confidence to feed into my soul. When she came back around, I mimicked her carefree attitude. It was enough to get me going, her son enthusiastically shouting encouragement and riding his little bike alongside me. While the sun shone, I felt a rush of hope.

When the ElliptiGO arrived in January, so too had the fires in Australia which killed the land and wildlife as well as people. COVID-19 raged throughout the world and by the end of February the death toll had reached the thousands. 10 months into planning, the hopes and dreams of 2020 being a year of prosperity were fast becoming a distant memory. I found myself weeping for those I did not know, consumed by a grief I couldn't quantify or justify. In my last book, A Culture of Kindness, I explored the idea that when the worst things prevail in society, when our backs are up against the wall, people come together. It's as if we know that we can't do this alone – that in fact we do need each other. Kindness with all its underlying values of gratitude, time, empathy, trust, connection, integrity and courage suddenly and quite naturally become the most important things of all.

I cautiously watched each new update. By May, France had closed its borders for the foreseeable future, and anyone entering the country had to go into two weeks of isolation to stop the spread of the virus. It made the idea of starting in England and going to France, let alone 19 other countries, impossible. Although the rules were changing every day in line with new data, none appeared to work in favour of the original concept. I had been planning for over a year and it felt like I was back to square one. Outwardly, I was disappointed. It had been a long, hard slog to get to a destination that felt like nowhere. Something internal sighed with relief. I just wasn't sure it was all worth it.

There seemed to be an umbrella of impending doom hanging over the 2020 challenge, but so much time and effort had already been spent that I wasn't prepared to let go. I couldn't simply abandon all the work.

When I drilled down to my feelings, I realised most of the work so far had been around securing long-term relationships. What became evident to me was those relationships were the key to the preparation phase. The rest, you could pretty much do on the back foot. When I reflected back, I realised that this was what I had done on the 500 mile walk I completed the previous year. I had packed a bag, and off I went. Not necessarily recommended, but more on that later. This challenge, however, was bigger. I had people relying on me to get this delivered. I had pushed the boundaries and for the first time since doing these challenges I was starting to question myself. Could I actually pull this off?

I needed to start again, but to do this I needed an idea. I had just three months to re-plan the entire challenge and keep the sponsors and supporters happy. I did what I always do – I called people and asked questions.

Asking people questions is often the most underrated of activities. We could stop wars with a few timely questions. Moving the whole challenge to stay within the bounds of the UK during the highs and lows of COVID-19 was huge, but it felt easier somehow and with the mood of the nation, it seemed appropriate to 'stay home' and share the message of kindness.

I decided to set off on 1st August, providing the UK COVID-19 laws would allow me to, of course. COVID aside, finding a route that covered the 5,000 miles required for the World Record was a challenge. Eventually I settled on going through every city in the UK. Starting in Truro, the most southern city, the route would zig zag up through the country (including Southern Ireland), ending up in Inverness. The only problem was that the route was only 4,500 miles long. So, I got in touch with Chris, a guy who I met in a small shop in Bath during my 2019 challenge. We had been in touch only a handful of times, but I reached out to him to see if he was interested in helping out.

"So, what do you think?" I asked. "I'm still 500 miles short, but something will come up to cover it, I think."

"Why don't you end on some Strava Art?" he said. "You could write KINDNESS across England."

"Yes, that is brilliant. Absolute genius." I knew instantly that it was what I would do. I didn't know how, but by then, I'd learnt that everything is possible.

By March, you didn't need to be spiritual guru to sense the UK had elevated its energetic vibration. You could feel it everywhere you went. I saw it in people's eyes as I passed them on the street – they had a growing sense of fear towards an unknown future. The sun rose and set exactly the same as any other day, but we were confined to the four walls of our homes. My speaking gigs were cancelled, and yet this gave me little understanding of how the rest of the world was affected. Those with spaces to smell the flowers and feel the sun verses those who lived in small, confined flats. Those who had work they could do from home and those who didn't. People who had children and those who didn't. Those in relationships that were already teetering on the edge. Everyone had a story to add to the human library. But beyond the fear there was something else that I could physically see. It was kindness, masked in hope. And from that kindness, came gratitude.

Kindness began to sweep through the country, not just on social media or a meme but in real-life interactions. People spoke to each other in the street (within the social distancing rules), neighbours spoke to neighbours they had never interacted with before; exchanging details and asking if they needed anything. You could hear the conversations were softer, building connections, checking welfare. The tone was changing.

It was the gratefulness that followed, not only for the medical staff but for the people doing all the jobs that keep us functioning as a society (the truck drivers, the carers, the shop assistants, the rubbish collectors, the post people... The list is endless). Fear was transforming into unity. Suddenly with very little warning, we were brought back to a simpler life. The people who had been taken for granted were suddenly pushed into the limelight. You could hear the country clapping for the National Health Service and see the tears people shed for the unknown. Life was scary for many. Fear swept through our communities like a hurricane, but we united in that, weathering the storm... Some more than others.

Communities pushed back on the negative, eager to hear stories of hope and have something to follow that was greater than themselves. Our future, for the most part, had been taken for granted. We all need something bigger than ourselves to focus our minds: a beautiful garden, trees, food grown from the earth, children raised to be well rounded and happy. Many people had already had that wake-up call and understood that there is such a short time available to ensure our lives have purpose.

Life in the age of COVID has changed many people's mindsets. After living with less, people realised that their happiness actually improved. Life could return to the same as before, but it wouldn't lead to the illusive happiness that people have been seeking since time began. Others went the opposite way, stockpiling goods, clearing entire supermarket shelves and causing an outcry from those left with nothing. This inner fear is as old as humanity itself – the need to protect ourselves and have what we need to survive. We have evolved so much but have forgotten that we really only need very little. In days gone by, we were much more self-sufficient. We grew our own food and lived off of the land. Now, we rely on a sea of commercialism to keep us afloat, and never had this change in society become more evident than when the pandemic hit and the wheels of capitalism ground to a halt.

Months later, I could feel the UK shift again when they went from idolising our politicians to vilifying them. The movement from love to hate swept like waves in a storm, you never quite knew what would be hit next. The media, of course, played a huge part in that, but it was us, the people, who were like drops in the ocean, all moving together wherever we were led. I was less concerned with the hate itself but more with how it grew, the blame and shame unstoppable in its velocity. If just one social media post or one news article can cause societal change, then we are in a danger much greater than the pandemic. We're in danger of ourselves.

Lockdown gave me some much-needed time to complete the jobs I had been putting off, so that by late spring, for the first time in as long as I can remember, I could stop ticking things off my to-do list. I felt no guilt at all. Instead, I decided to enjoy the warm afternoons and dusted off the cushions for the garden bench.

Before spring had even sprung, the garden began to hint at summer. The insects buzzed in the air and every day of the week felt like an easy Sunday from the 1980s. It reminded me of William Henry Davies' poem, Leisure.

*What is this life if, full of care,*
*We have no time to stand and stare*
*No time to stand beneath the boughs*
*And stare as long as sheep or cows*
*No time to see, when woods we pass,*
*Where squirrels hide their nuts in grass*
*No time to, in broad daylight,*
*Streams full of stars, like skies at night.*
*No time to turn at Beauty's glance*
*And watch her feet, how they can dance*
*No time to wait till her mouth can*
*Enrich that smile her eyes began,*
*A poor life this if, full of care*
*We have no time to stand and stare.*

As I lay down on one hazy afternoon, my head sinking into the cushion, I remember noticing how perfect the temperature was. No breeze, no stifling heat, just perfect. Instead of feeling like I had to tick off my list, I enjoyed reading and took an afternoon nap in the shade of the house.

These moments, moments where I have things to do but don't do them, come into my life very infrequently. Before 2020, I rarely ever stopped to take time for myself. These balmy afternoons were a chance to stop and stare, to recalibrate what was important. I had been so busy seeking that I forgot what I was looking for. The truth is, it was right in front of me all along.

Mostly though, as I lay in the garden sun and appreciated the simple fact of life, I took stock of how far removed I felt from the person I had been on my first challenge: climbing Kilimanjaro just six months after Paul had died.

# Chapter 3

## Kilimanjaro: 2012

### "Not far now."

"I just have to walk up a hill for a few days very slowly," I told myself. "How hard can it be?" How wrong I was.

I looked down at my brown walking boots, comfortingly familiar in such an unfamiliar place. Just six months after meeting the stranger walking his dog on the beach, I was climbing Kilimanjaro.

A colleague of Paul's decided to climb Kilimanjaro in his memory and had asked if I would like to join him. In my usual fashion, I said yes, with no real understanding of the challenge ahead of me. You may think this was a huge leap in such a short space of time, and you wouldn't be wrong. I can barely remember it. It was the fastest and the slowest six months of my life.

The path continued upwards, my breath laboured, my steps small and slow. I kept climbing, using tree roots as footholds. The ground underfoot was worn by the many feet to have trodden the brown soil path before me. I could see just far enough ahead to enjoy the beauty surrounding me, but not far enough to be daunted by what lay ahead.

I had never attempted anything like this, so before we left I had no real understanding of the physical and mental demands. I quickly realised I didn't enjoy training. After completing many more challenges, I can now see the benefits of careful preparation, but at the time reaching the summit felt so far away that I struggled to realise how important it was.

Although I had barely put any time into training, I put hours into rallying interest in the story. I wanted to share who Paul was. We got his old workplace involved and each of his colleagues held fundraising days. I got the press interested, encouraging people to share the Just Giving page across social media. In the end, we raised around £14,000. This was all before I had even taken a step or got on the flight. However, in the end, things did not go to plan.

As I walked, if I looked down to my right, I could see streams running below me through the forest, the sound of water was music to my ears, keeping the whole forest alive. I focused on the rhythm of my wheezing, the heaviness in my chest and the steady and consistent footsteps of the guide ahead. I was still grieving, taking mementos of Paul with me, wearing his clothes and needing to feel as close to him as possible. I wanted him to walk with me, if only in spirit, and the guide humoured me with no judgement.

The guide didn't judge my need to talk about the memory of the dead man he had never known and my reasons for doing the climb. He was kind. He had done this thousands of times and I was just another person with another story.

I only just managed to keep up with my guide. I had read that you needed to walk very slowly to avoid altitude sickness. So, because I am not keen on fitness of any kind, I used this as an excuse to train by walking very slowly on a treadmill. I know! Running very fast would perhaps have been better training, but hey ho, despite what some may think, I always look for the easiest option.

We were approximately half a mile behind the larger group, partly through choice and partly because most of my training had been done taking tiny steps on a treadmill rather than in muscle building exercises. I was a novice adventurer, in my own mind; I still am. But I know those that think they can't, won't, and if I can, then anyone can.

Throughout the morning I had a chance to ask the guide about his family and the life he had carved out for himself.

"So, do you have family?" "Yes, I have my father, my mother is no longer here. I have three brothers. There are four of us. We are all building a house at the moment. We bring our money together and work together."

His English was excellent but had a bluntness to its form. I had to try hard not to mimic his accent.

"Oh, that sounds good," I said encouragingly, even though I knew little of the life he had endured to get to that place of unity. "Yes, we are fortunate," he replied thoughtfully. "More fortunate than most in this country."

We continued to talk about the country and its people, and about his wife and new baby. He said he knew the UK gave aid to other countries through charities and such like, but that this was mostly intercepted before it reached those in need. This struck me the most about all the things we talked about, and this new knowledge caused a knot of sadness in my stomach, an uneasiness at the human condition and frustration at those who justified that it was somehow ok to take from the poor for their own personal gain. This stayed at the surface of my thoughts as I looked up at the canopy cover, so thick and dense. The sun trickled down, like water between rocks, through the deep green of the forest.

To the left of me the ground fell away, the trees descending down the slope dripping with creepers and connected by miles of cobwebs which caught the dappled light that snuck through the branches. To my right, the darkness of the forest was more prevalent, but then, in that dark, we spotted a rare flower. Lit by a single beam of light, the bloom looked like a small orchid, alone in a sea of shadows and greenery. It was as though someone was holding a torch to it. Just a single, perfectly formed pink flower with thick, strong, dark green leaves. I had never seen a flower so perfect. It felt like an important moment.

"I hope the others ahead saw it," the guide said, as if we were the luckiest people in the world.

I knew it was a moment I needed to treasure. We can stand in the shadows or we can choose to step into the light so that the world can see us in all our glory. We all need to be more like that pink flower.

As I continued walking, I became more aware of a throbbing pain in my right big toe and by the time I limped into the large open grassy clearing where we would camp for the night, I was in complete agony. The camp was light and felt a world away from the surrounding forest that we had spent the whole day walking through. I removed my boots, expecting to see something gruesome, but there wasn't anything obviously sinister looking. The nail had dug into my skin and had become infected. I won't go into details but after some pretty brutal work on the nail I managed to release the pressure.

The camp was divided off into huts. I took a hot water bottle and went to where all the guides were preparing food and getting ready for the next day so I could get some hot water. I spent time chatting with the guides and people who were local to the area as they invited me to drink the native tea with them. I remember enjoying their company even with the pain of my toe. I felt valued, cared for and loved. I was grateful although my mind sat firmly in the sadness of the past and the impending future. I wanted to stay with them, these real people, with no pretence or sense of materialism. But I knew this was their time, to be themselves without being 'on the job', so I headed off to bed, feeling envious.

Remembrance Day came and went. We had decided to complete the climb for a well-known charity that helped injured veterans. Paul was ex-army and wore a wrist band with the name of the charity. He spoke with his army mates and when chinooks passed overhead, he was always mesmerised and taken to a place of nostalgia that I could never truly understand. He had adjusted to civilian life better than most, but the journey had not been the smoothest. He had called the transition his 'mid-life crisis'. I had taken a poppy to commemorate those fallen. It seemed even more pertinent this year.

It took four days to get to basecamp, moving up the mountain slowly and with consideration. The tall trees provided shadows and shade as we continued up the path made by thousands of other footsteps. A flicker, an unusual movement in the trees, forced me to stop. A monkey swung onto a branch to take a look at what was passing. We moved on, and the land opened back up. It barely looked like there was an incline amid the vast landscape.

I continued walking, keeping pace with the guide as much as possible. Across a vast, flat piece of land basecamp came into sight, the mountain top sat somewhere in the distant clouds. I knew that after some rest, I would be climbing through the night. My breath caught in my chest at the thought of it. On the final steps to basecamp, I wrote words with stones, messages of love. I was in a world of nostalgia and my head was not really in the game. I would later discover that this would be to my detriment.

I started to feel altitude sickness and by the time we reached the huts I was severely nauseous and struggled to breathe. We had a total of six hours to rest until midnight, when we would finish the final stage of the climb in pitch black; the ground steep and unsteady underfoot. We were promised, if the clouds and weather were on our side, the reward of a sunrise we would never forget.

When the guides came to wake everyone, I was already awake and feeling terrible. The sense of not being able to breathe freely was debilitating. It not only put me in a 'fear for life' state, but I recognised that completing a physical challenge with only half of my lung capacity put me at a considerable disadvantage. Add the sickness, the infected toe and training that was, well let's be honest, as much use as a chocolate kettle, I knew this was going to be a pretty brutal six hours.

I was wearing all the clothes I had bought with me underneath Paul's green, army issue jacket that was still too big even with all my extra layers. He had loved this jacket and it followed him wherever he went. It was one more thing to make me feel closer to him, another thing that screamed 'he's still here'.

Outside in the darkness, the temperature was beyond freezing, the drinking water bottles forming ice cores. Every part of my body was covered, with just my eyes peeping out. If I was to try to create a picture for you, I was the Michelin man walking up a blooming big mountain in the pitch dark.

I felt it in the pit of my stomach, a sickness, a light headedness where my body and my mind felt as if they were detaching, a mix of feeling both full and incredibly hungry. Everything a contradiction. Eating at this point was almost impossible but necessary, I knew I was not getting enough calories, but I had to push on with the group. I stood just outside the door of the wooden hut and put on my head torch, checking I had everything I might need for the night of walking. The altitude sickness was constant and not improving.

A roar of noise from the guides indicated we were due to start zig zagging our way up, and off we went. I kept my head down. *Follow the person in front, watch their shoes and keep going.* I could feel the ground was soft underfoot.

About an hour passed with the glare of my head torch hitting the back of the person in front's shoes. I looked up for a moment and could see the lights of the head torches snaking up the mountain ahead of me. Strings of people, moving together to reach the summit, just to catch a glimpse of an unforgettable sunrise.

I continued upwards, drawing comfort from the lights on the occasions I gave myself a chance to look up. The line stopped for a moment while people refuelled and drank the water that had not yet frozen. I took a second to look up at the darkness of the sky in the hope that Paul would, from wherever he was, somehow relieve me of the discomfort I was feeling. The sky was so full of stars it would have made the sun jealous. It was as if the sky could become a single bright white canvas, more and more stars appearing the longer I looked. They were so close I could almost have reached out and touched them. This sky seemed unseen and unspoilt, something more beautiful than I would ever see again. Either that, or I was hallucinating from the altitude and lack of food and sleep.

We continued walking for a few more hours and reached a large rock formation where a few people had taken refuge. It was just me and the guide now – the rest of the group were further on ahead. I felt like someone had turned my body inside out. My energy was low, I could feel the fever taking over, and while I tried to eat something, I just wanted to be sick. My mind kept saying: *You can't do this; you can't do this. You aren't good enough. You didn't train hard enough. You aren't ready for this.*

In the end, I allowed my mind to win. I wearily sank down onto the rocks, totally and utterly exhausted.

"I'm done," I said to no one in particular. The guide turned his kind brown eyes on me.

"I'm sorry," I said to him, my own eyes filling with hopeless tears, "I'm just not able to go any further."

I'd weighed up the options. I could continue to the top for three more hours with the potential of completely losing my ability to breathe whilst simultaneously throwing up, having to cut my toe off and leaving behind various frozen-off extremities. Or, I could head back in the hope I didn't need to give back the £14,000 I'd raised. In that moment I didn't care, I was done and ready to go back.

The guide looked at me, heard what I said, and said nothing for a moment. He crouched down next to me, looking me deep in the eyes. In the end, he stood up and simply waved me on. He could see I had more in me, that it was my mind and not my body that was holding me back. Now, looking back, he was right.

"Not far now," he said, "and we will be there."

So much meaning in those few words. So much belief, so much hope.

His words were enough to balance my mind, to give recognition and hope, to let me know he believed in me, even if I didn't. That might be the greatest gift we can ever give someone: belief. It is the very epitome of kindness. I don't remember much of the rest of the climb. We often block out the parts of our lives that are too much for us, and this was one of those times.

The soft sand we had walked over for what felt like a lifetime turned rocky. As I climbed, my thickly gloved hands grappled for solid handholds to pull myself up. Then, the darkness started to lift, so slowly it was almost imperceptible. The light rose and peeked over the horizon, hinting at the closeness of the summit. With still an hour to go, the light brought energy and hope to know warmth and comfort was near. A feeling of relief washed over me, as I realised, I would not be held in the dark and the cold forever.

My mind had been distracted long enough to stop focusing on the sickness and it finally subsided. The voices in my head were drowned out by something more powerful: belief.

Looking down on the clouds, sat on the edge of a rocky outcrop, we watched as the sun rose, just me and the guide who I had spent four days with. I had listened to his life story and he had heard mine. It was a wonder to me, to be sat there, on top of the world yet still unable to quantify what it was all about. I took pictures, went through the motions, and sat like the marshmallow man's little sister on the side of the mountain. wondering how the hell I was going to get down.

This time, instead of zig zagging with great care back down the rocks to the sandy paths, I ran down the centre of the slope arm in arm with one of the girls from the group, trying to drown out the pain of my muscles with adrenalin.

The sun shone down on us and I remember thinking; *well, that was easy!* We were down in no time, but the path of least resistance doesn't always come easily. Running down a sandy hill for 20 minutes with very little muscle and no fuel in my body had a pretty detrimental effect. By the end of the first day of descent I had jarring pains throughout my entire body and was barely able to put my foot down to take steps. I was running a high temperature, my skin felt like it was crawling. I was feverish and the altitude sickness was back with a vengeance. The nausea laughed in the face of my short respite at the summit. Now it was time for payback.

A few hours after everyone else, I eventually made it to the next camp. I was now unable to hold food down and was drifting in and out of a state of awareness of what was going on around me. The guide suggested I lie down for a while. I felt myself dream, floating in and out of consciousness, not quite sure what I could do to try and feel better.

My guide came back and woke me.

"Glad you are awake. I think I come back and maybe you would be dead," he said straight faced. "How are you now?"

"Still not good. Maybe I feel sicker. Fever is worse." He pondered me for a moment and then said, "I come back."

He returned with some other guides, taking my blood pressure and deciding to carry me down the hill on a stretcher. They moved quickly and I could hear them chatting to me and sometimes to themselves. It was comforting. I felt safe and as if everything was going to be ok.

I can't remember much of the journey back down the mountain that night, except a huge overwhelming sense of gratefulness. I just remember thinking; *I'm not going to die.* By the time we reached the hotel, I still felt pretty rough, but I was able to function. My head felt like I was reliving my first ever hangover from University, and I slept fitfully in a heightened sense of fear and unease.

The following morning, I booked a flight back and left the hotel before the rest of the group returned. All the money that I had, I left as a tip for the guides. Then, I was off.

The airport was like any other, full of excitement, a buzz like nowhere else in the world. I checked in, went through passport control, and walked into the bright, white terminal; my head still heavy with the dull ache that follows a migraine. I breathed a sigh of relief, watching the people milling around, wondering what their stories were. Were they grieving too? Were they excited? Was this a once in a lifetime trip for them? Where were they going? Were they in love? Were they happy? I would never know.

I sat on the airport floor feeling entirely spent, mentally and physically exhausted. I remember thinking, *thank god that's over. I won't be in a hurry to do that again.* I was safe and there was comfort in that. I had reached the summit with a body that was not ready, and a mind that had not been trained and that I could not control. Still in the depths of my grief I was trying to find a way to live again: I had climbed a mountain, literally and figuratively.

After returning to the UK I got in touch with the charity we had raised the money for and asked them what they would do with it. I wanted to be able to say, "This is what was done in Paul's memory."

I felt in some strange way, as thousands of others have before me, that I could create a legacy. I wanted something good to come out of the tragedy of his death.

The charity's response was that it had gone into 'the big pot' and it could not be tracked. I was astounded. Was that it? Was Paul's memory put down to an amount of money that in the end, had no set purpose? I didn't want his memory to be so vague. Over the coming weeks I realised I had made a mistake. I had attempted to put a figure on a memory. That was not what we were about, and it was not what his memory should encompass.

I realised chasing money to honour Paul's memory did not sit comfortably with me. Paul and I stood for acceptance of each other, and total honesty even when it hurt. We stood by each other and when I wanted to walk alone, as was my default, he never let me. He retold stories of the 'good things' he had done, in the hope that through 'good karma' he would hopefully see positive things in the cycle of life and beyond.

I found there was a discrepancy in the charity sector: the need to do good versus meeting monetary targets. The money always seemed to win. I just couldn't understand why the organisations wouldn't bring more likeminded people together, rather than pay people to hit fundraising targets of hundreds of thousands of pounds. Charities have become more 'business' than most conventional corporations.

Of course, charities need money to run, but how much? Do they need to decorate offices to make sure they're 'on brand' at a cost of thousands of pounds, painstakingly raised by supporters who trust that their donations will be spent on the causes these charities talk so passionately about. We need to look for smarter options to achieve what needs to be done, with less expense. Sadly, I could not see big charities doing that. So, I decided to create Sunshine People.

Sunshine People would be a social movement that promoted kindness over money. I would carry on doing yearly challenges in Paul's memory, but instead of raising money, I would instead simply ask people to donate acts of kindness to strangers.

You might ask, "What is the point? Sponsorship is for raising money!"

However, what I wanted to do was question the norm. People so often blindly raise money for a chosen charity, taking pleasure that they have done their bit. Giving without thought, with the click of a few buttons or by digging into our pockets to throw some change into a bucket, gives us the idea that we have done enough. However, the interactions are small and often they hold no deeper emotional meaning. When you give money, you do not get to see the eyes of someone who is grateful for the time you gave to listen, or the effect of a smiling friendly face when someone's world is so lonely that they wonder how they can carry on. The impact of an emotional exchange sits with both the giver and the receiver for longer than any amount of money.

Please don't misunderstand me, I do donate, but I no longer give blindly. I am very wary of, and avoid, engaging with charities that squander money and carefully cook the percentages to 'prove' they have not overspent on overheads.

Consider this for a moment: if all our interactions continue to be measured by money, how can we focus on each other first? Positive and kind human interactions have become an aspiration, instead of the norm. We do not expect to help our neighbours and in most cities, you might not even know who those neighbours are. With the ability to travel and the world getting smaller and smaller, our communities have changed dynamically and with that the natural chance to be kind has diminished. Again, as you read this you may say, "I know my neighbour and I was kind just yesterday." This isn't a personal attack. What I mean is, historically, we focus more on money since the age of capitalism. We have been made to feel as if we need more things, and so the money conversation in our minds is always a loud one.

I would love to see large charities questioning how they do things, finding better ways to achieve their goals without wasting large amounts of money, and to show more care and appreciation for fundraisers. I have example after example of charities accepting sponsorship money without providing kindly support, thanks or even acknowledgement to the person who raised it. Some charities are just businesses with tax breaks. Sunshine People was born to buck the trend and encourage people to consider a more human focused approach. Don't get me wrong, I need business sponsorship to help keep Sunshine People going, but I've learnt to make a little go a long way.

Setting up Sunshine People has not been a smooth journey, but it has been an interesting one. Over the years I have seen an increase in the understanding of the mission. Some people no longer want to give money to charities as they have already been stung. Instead, they want to know the memory of someone is valued above currency.

Some eight years later, when it was all going spectacularly wrong on the ElliptiGO, hope was given to me in the form of extreme generosity powered by a mutual desire to share the message of kindness.

# Chapter 4

# ElliptiGO World Record challenge: 2020

## "Training involves the mind"

When planning any challenge there is an uncomfortable moment when you don't know if all the things you need will come together. Will people come forward, the right people, the faces that will make this a success? Will we get the funds and items we need? If we can't gather those, will it matter? Who will be affected? I was working hard not to impact others, everything hanging in the balance with the self-imposed weight of the task sitting firmly on my own shoulders. By mid-June, after months of work, it finally felt like things were coming together and I started to see some progress.

I would lose myself at times, staring into space and wondering. Dread would rise up through my stomach to my head and I would have to physically shake myself, giving myself a reminder to breathe. How would I get to a place where I was comfortable with the endless days and physical exhaustion? How would I find the sheer determination I would need to actually finish this challenge? These questions could impact my ability to achieve.

While cycling across America I broke my 3,000-mile target into smaller, more manageable chunks, just concentrating on a single day at a time. Then, when the 60 miles a day seemed too much, I would break it down again with hourly goals, only thinking about what was manageable.

For my ElliptiGO journey, once I was at the start in Truro, I would just think about the next city. And then the city after that. I needed to remember that this was so much bigger than me riding an ElliptiGO, it was about sharing a message that was becoming ever more important in the divisiveness that society was moving towards.

This particular challenge was different from my cycle across America on many levels. One, the weather in the UK was unlikely to be on my side at that time of year. Two, this time there would be no flat Florida in the basking sun to enjoy, only hills and British rain. Three, it was four months of riding every day – twice as long as the previous challenge. Four, it was a World Record attempt on a stand-up bike.

I really needed to start to get into my own head, to make a pattern and belief system that would make this immense challenge feel remotely achievable. About six months before leaving for the challenge I gave a talk at the 'Words by the Water' event in the Lake District. It was the weekend that the world started shutting down due to COVID-19. While there, I heard the well-known cyclist, Emily Chappell, speak. She talked about cycling across Europe as part of the Transcontinental race. As she shared how she had trained her mind, how she dealt with all of the obstacles that came her way, I was in awe. This was what proper adventurers looked like. People who slept by the side of the road and then got up and rode another 100 miles up sheer mountains. Emily shared what she thought about during these moments: her idols, the women who she looked up to and admired. She explained how she broke down her challenges to manageable bits. But my favourite tip, and the simplest, was her 'snack pots' mounted to the front of the bike. I knew if I was doing one thing first, snack pots were it.

How would I really dive deep into changing my mindset before the task, but also on the road? How would I stop the wave of dread that overcame me so unexpectedly? I made up stories, reframing what I believed or had been conditioned to believe. Tuning out the sceptics to hear my own voice would be my saving grace.

I wanted to make this challenge part of my life. It wasn't unusual, it was just something that I was doing.

The first thing I did was imagine that I was simply taking on a temporary job. My job was to ride my ElliptiGO for seven hours a day, the same as anyone else doing their nine to five. When the rain came, I would remind myself there were lots of road maintenance and outdoor workers who had to endure the same conditions, but I got to have changing scenery as I went along so I was lucky.

The second thing I did was make the ElliptiGO my best friend. The idea that I was doing this alone didn't bother me when I thought about it during training, but I was aware that until I was on the ride I wouldn't really know for sure. Many people would say, "Won't you be lonely?" and "Wow, you're doing it alone?"

So, I had to build a relationship with the bike. I needed to want to be with the bike. It was no longer a thing but someone who needed my company, too. I named her Charis; meaning goddess of kindness, and it was up to me to help Charis fulfil her destiny. She wanted to see the world and be something greater than just a chunk of metal and gears. It sounds bonkers, but I felt that at this point anything that might help was worth trying.

I also knew I needed to make the challenge pleasurable. I'd been told that there was so much that could go wrong or be difficult. So many people focused on the negative. I needed to tune into things that made me happy. So, the third thing I did was list all the things I was going to enjoy when I was on Charis (even when the weather was not on my side). I would listen to all 300 plus Tough Girl podcast episodes, I would spend time continuing to learn through my love of audio books, I would get to see every city in the UK and take in all that beautiful scenery and coast lines. I am not sure many could say that. Charis and I would indirectly be generating acts of kindness that we would never even know about. It would be easy to make up those stories to help when motivation waned.

I dug deep and started to find solutions to the things that caused the 'dread wave', as I came to know it. However, as quickly as my hope rose it fell. Some of the equipment still had not arrived, a significant sponsor pulled out due to COVID and I slept restlessly wondering if I could really pull this off. I dragged my mind back to my three belief systems, training my brain as much as I could. Would it be enough?

I organised for film students to video the challenge which required a support vehicle and all the associated costs, and as the students didn't drive a driver was also needed. We would use the vehicle as a place to sleep and generally as a place to be. In truth, this added extra pressure, but it felt important for others to be part of the challenge.

Phone calls arrived with bad news; emails didn't arrive with the answers I was relying on. The key things I really needed to happen were out of my hands. Promises were broken. But I kept powering through. I was so in my own head I couldn't even see the outside world; it was blurring into one. I couldn't see the change in seasons or take in the smells of summer. Being let down but still getting up and persevering felt beyond my control, as though someone else was powering me on through the setbacks.

When asked where this perseverance comes from, there is no short answer. I inherited a tenacity I never asked for, but I'm also quick to walk away from things when the time calls. I do not hold onto things that do not serve me or others well. Keeping going on this challenge and all my other challenges is about purpose. If it was just for me, maybe I would have stopped, but this was for a bigger, more important message. Something greater than money, it matched my values and my need to inspire others.

When Paul died, I learnt not to be frightened of completely immersing myself in my grief. It is the same for everything we do. We have to feel the bottom of every situation to feel the elation of the wonders of life. We can't enjoy the top of the mountain without having climbed from the bottom.

Paul believed in me. He was sometimes frightened of the love, as was I, as we all are. He would have stood by my side and made me believe the impossible was possible. Maybe it's not my own tenacity at all. Maybe it's his spirit powering me along, and the memory of man who loved me more than I have ever known.

I was beyond tired. Emotionally, I was on the ropes. But still I continued. I emailed sponsors, looking for a ray of hope that maybe the big resources I needed would eventually come through. I just needed to get to the right person. It is how I imagine a gambling addict must feel... Just one more email and it might be the one. Then, in tears, and wondering if it was in fact achievable, I'd gain a new connection that gave me new hope. The main funding was still missing, but I knew that I was putting everything into the search and there was nothing more I could do. I just had to stay optimistic, but it didn't stop the feeling that nothing was going to plan.

When I was feeling the most exhausted, there was still a tiny ball of energy bouncing around my body like a pinball that kept me going, to keep working, to keep asking. I sat for 14 hours each day in the chair where I had been sitting when I was told I wouldn't have the sponsorship I'd expected. One day, sat in my usual spot, I got a call to say a friend's business would provide the sponsorship required. Everything I had been holding onto, all the anguish and dread… All of it stopped. There was just my friend telling me that she believed in what I was doing. She saw me, supported me and accepted me for who I was and all that I did.

A wave of deep relief washed over my body in slow motion. As it worked from my head to my toes, the tears came. I wept tears of hope and stress and love and gratitude. I was sat in that same place, the same chair, but my circumstances had changed exponentially. It was a deep reminder to me that in the end, optimism and hope would always help find a way.

Ready to give up everything to make the challenge work, I decided to sell all of my belongings. I stood outside in a small, sunny field lined with shipping containers and unlocked the familiar green box which contained my life. As I opened the door, all my worldly belongings stared back at me, the memories of my past swirling through my mind as items revealed themselves. The blanket box inherited from my grandmother, framed pictures of friends, Paul and myself as a child. My entire life in physical form, everything from beds to trinkets collected over years. They had been sat in a container for far too long and I realised it served no purpose. Knowing I needed more funding for this trip, I was left with no option. I moved through the container, taking pictures of items to set up a 'container sale'.

As I was clearing things out, I got to thinking about how much value we put on material things. We protect things which spend most of their life in a cupboard never being used or seen with such fear of losing them. They feed a part of our brain that will never be satisfied. I knew now that I needed less. Less to worry about breaking, less to take care of and worry about getting mouldy or lost. As each item was picked up by a new stranger and the container slowly emptied, I was uplifted by the removal of 'things' cluttering my life. I packed a last carload of personal items. Everything else was gone.

It felt like this act was so intrinsically linked with the challenges, to start a conversation on how we interact and behave in all areas of society, to measure by kindness and not money or things, and consider kindness not as something fluffy but imperative. I wanted to encourage more people to consider the way they interact in workplaces, families, society, politics and communities; including myself.

Mid-July, with two weeks to go, it was so easy to focus on all the things that hadn't happened yet. There had been a constant evolution of change, days where everything I had been working on was cancelled or rejected and I'd have to 'pivot' in a new direction. In all the challenges I have completed, something has gone wrong, so I've learnt how to navigate these hiccups. Subsequently I can take to new approaches faster and more seamlessly. However, this challenge, well, it was throwing me against brick walls at 100mph and I was absolutely exhausted before I had even started. I decided that it would be easier in so many ways once I was at the starting point in Truro with my ElliptiGO, just the open road ahead of me. Nothing more could be done at that point.

Then, with just 10 days to go before the start, the pinball machine started up again in my body. The support van broke down and the support driver had found a new job meaning he was no longer able to come along. In so many ways it would have been easier to go alone but I had made a commitment to the students, so I needed to find alternative arrangements. This value of loyalty was pressing on me. Although I was eating five meals a day for training, I was in the most part powered by adrenaline alone. How would I find a solution? In the end when I was at my wits end wondering what I would do, a dear friend's partner stepped up and saved the day. They bought a small van with a tiny kitchen that slept two comfortably and four less so. I put my trust in the world again and put a post out onto social media asking for people to be a support driver for the vehicle and, as usual, hoped for the best.

The preparation over the past months had been all consuming. Sara, one my closest friends who has known me for twenty years, has always been a light in my life. She stands by me loyally even when she doesn't understand the plans that I make and as we have grown up (well, attempted to) we have grown differently but respected each other for it. She hasn't always seen the worst or best parts of my life due to distance, and I haven't always seen hers, but we understand them and feel them as if it were our very own lives. She is my go-to, and my life would be poorer for not having her in it. She is my chosen family. That evening we packed the van in the evening sun, with views of Dorset around of us. Life seemed sweeter with a beer that's drunk between getting the tasks completed for the next day. D day had arrived.

I hadn't slept well. I knew there were other things I needed to do, things that would make me feel more confident about pulling this off, but I had run out of time. I chose the day before leaving to make two Tarte Tatins. One for some friends of the family, and another for Sara and her partner who had been so supportive.

The day before I left my mother watched me making the tarts and she said, "Maybe you should prioritise the things that are more important to get the challenge ready." I popped the tarts into the oven. "Nope, this is what I am doing, it makes me happy."

Of course, she was right, but to me this was important. For me, saying thank you and being able to give back in any way was more important than anything else. If something was to happen to me, I would know people had my time and effort as a gift. Nothing will ever be more important than that. I enjoy cooking, it's a stress reliever – something that I do that is not work, just something that produces joy for others and myself. I needed more of that. Maybe we all do.

I was up at six on the morning to do all the last-minute things I needed to before leaving, but I was shattered and hadn't slept properly in weeks. Luckily, I was already at a decent stage of preparedness: the food was packed, the van sorted, the equipment loaded and charged ready for use. All my belongings from the container were sold.

I was as ready as I would ever be.

# Chapter 5

## ElliptiGO World Record challenge: 2020

## "...and so it begins."

I looked up at the small church-like cathedral in Truro, cobbled streets surrounding me. For a summer's day in Cornwall, England, it was cold: the sort of cold that seeps straight into your bones. The idea of what lay ahead over the next four months felt so huge I had to squash the thoughts down, make them teeny tiny and not allow them in, because when I did, they took my breath away.

*It's just a temporary job, it's just a temporary job.* I repeated the words over and over in my mind. Echoing back, came, *I'm not good enough, I'm not capable, I'm not an adventurer, I have no idea what I'm doing.* The doubts whispered in the wind, trying to knock me off course. But there could be no backing out. When the wind blows, we have no choice but to stand tall regardless.

I knew that whilst I could have been more prepared, starting the challenge on the 1st August in the UK's most southerly city, I had no choice but to use the resources I had. Internally, I dug deep and drew on hope upon hope that I might pull this off.

It was later in the day than planned when I set off and the climbs were much worse than I had imagined. The bike simply would not get up them, or more to the point, I could not get up them. It was a sad fact that I was more physically prepared than I had been for any other challenge and I still wasn't good enough. The cool wind and my inner doubts chilled me to the bone.

Eventually, after 5,000 feet of elevation and 30 miles into the daily 55-mile target, I found the support van, climbed in and slept. The exhaustion reminded me of my first day cycling across America. There was nothing left, my legs wouldn't move anymore. All I could do was lie down.

Sunshine People empowers people to project their creativity into the world with gusto, giving them an opportunity to take something forwards into society. I had spent the previous four months working with film students who applied to document the challenge as part of their university courses. Each week we had calls over Zoom about how they were getting on as I attempted to prepare them for what was to come. It was more to add to the ever-growing list of things I had to do in the lead up to the challenge. One of the students didn't drive and so a driver was also needed for the new support vehicle kindly bought just a week before the first day of the challenge.

The 'support' crew came, for the most part, from a catalogue of errors. In just one week a group of strangers came together, getting me off the ground and onto my mission to make the World Record and fuel the conversation on kindness. Before the challenge, we'd not met in person. It was heart-warming but also fraught with huge challenges.

Just one week to go until I had to be in Truro to start the challenge, the sound of every clock ticking haunted me. The weight of time sat heavy on me. The tightness in my chest threatened to combust me internally. I had reached out on social media for any support I could get, and the world bought me... Alison.

In-tune, emotionally intelligent and hilarious, Alison volunteered to coordinate the drivers and act as a support person. She took control of all of the spreadsheets, communication and groups, and only then did I realise how much I had been carrying. A shining light, she was the angel among the darkness in that final week of preparation. When the worst would happen, she was the person who turned it all around.

The support team continued to grow – a little community of people doing a few days here and there. Some worked out, some didn't have the resilience needed to problem solve under pressure: the challenge within the challenge. While it was difficult to organise, a community grew from it, greater than the challenge itself and with more lessons learnt.

Just a few days after the gruelling first day, the August sun shone brightly and led me down every sort of road and track. I pedalled through tall, beautiful trees in the Devonshire countryside, the track so bumpy it was nigh on impassable and then, gradually, it eventually disappeared. I hadn't noticed until I was no longer on it. I could hear traffic on the other side of some undergrowth but there was no way through. I called friends, and using the tracker, we tried to navigate back to the tantalisingly close road. Eventually I resigned myself to heading back the way I'd come. With time ticking, I walked Charis back and wondered how I had gotten so lost without realising. When things happen so gradually, we barely notice them at all, be it the decline of relationships, the road we travel down in life or the progress we see in our life's work. We all need to take a million tiny positive actions every day to keep us on the path to the goals we want to achieve. After a few more wrong turns, I realised the route planner was set to touring bike rather than road bike, and I got myself back on track.

I followed the flat roads out of Exeter along the river, knowing that the worst of the hills had been left behind in Cornwall. I started the day travelling along canal paths and stopped along the way to get witnesses to sign my notebook for the World Record evidence log. I love nothing more than to hear people's stories and this was a perfect reason to stop, listen and learn, but the clock continued to tick. I had to keep going. Every time I stopped; I was eating into time that I needed to reach my destination.

I travelled through Tiverton and past a pub that Paul and I used to visit. I wondered if I should take the time to stop, to sit and watch the river pass by, as we had done so many times before. I kept pedalling; time didn't allow for such sentimentality.

A few days later, I made it to Burrow Hump, ultimately a 10-minute steep climb to the top of a small and defined hill rewarded with the most stunning views overlooking Somerset. A patchwork of fields and life existed below me, its vastness unquantifiable. History oozed from every inch of ground I stepped on. I arrived back at the car park and noticed a larger than average transit, its back doors open, and a tall man stood surrounded by refreshments.

'That's an interesting machine, what are you doing?' He asked me.

I explained the mission: 5,000 miles, the World Record, four months, every city in the UK and the drive for kinder communities.

"So, what are you guys doing here?" I asked.

He, it turned out, was the support for a group of people who were cycling from Land's End to John O'Groats. My reaction was one of awe, "Wow that's tough going." He looked at me as though I had gone mad. "Are you joking, after what you're doing, that challenge is easy."

I thought about it, and I didn't know if it was. Land's End to John O Groats seemed to me so much harder. I guess like everything in life, perception is key.

Riding the sea front was a joy, through the Royal Victoria Park in Southampton and on. I was now hugging the coast, my favourite place to be. While challenging and painful, the miles built, and I pushed on through, the thing that concerned me more and more each day became the students and the people who had come to support me.

I kept trying to keep focus on the task in hand. Following the coast was a dream, despite the bumpy cycle tracks. The sun shone as I crossed over the river Hamble. I tried to remain calm and considered, knowing we had many nights with nowhere to stay coming up. There was so much at stake. An animated woman stopped her car next to me having seen the story in the news. She asked for a picture and I wanted to stop and chat more but, after the photo, I pushed on. With four cities and 48 miles to complete, the day was already going to be a close call and time was not on my side.

I looked out on the vast and beautiful sea and it gave me the energy I needed. I felt unbelievably grateful for the view, for the opportunity to see the world and to be able to do what I was doing. So, over the following days, while the pain in my legs grew under the pressure of the miles, I watched the soothing yellow fields with their neat, newly rolled hay bales pass by. All the world carried on with life, it kept going after everything that had happened to society. It reminded me: we are resilient. I am resilient.

By the time I got to London my skin had blistered in the heat and it was getting worse with each pedal. Nothing could be done so I kept plying on sun protection and hoping for the best. London was flat and the cycle paths were relatively quiet due to the government's ongoing advice to stay inside. The film student had joined me on a 'Boris bike' through London and then, in a park in London, she confessed that she had anxiety and was suffering from panic attacks. She had these before she came on the trip but hoped that by coming on the trip, she would find a way to deal with them. She no longer wanted to be there.

When I called the student's lecturer to update them, the response was:

"Yes, she had said to me a few weeks before she came that maybe she couldn't do it, but I said she should try. I convinced her she should do it."

Of course, I knew nothing about this. It was a reminder to me that honesty to and about ourselves is kindness. It is an important chance for the people around you to react and support accordingly. We could have put a different plan in place had I known. It was from this point that the catchphrase of the entire trip was born. *It is what it is.*

There is something empowering about accepting the circumstances we find ourselves in. Those simple words, *it is what it is*, remind us that we cannot change the situation. We may also find ourselves in a situation because of our own actions, but we always have to be willing to learn from it. I have learnt not only from the death of Paul but also the adventures I have been on, that so much anguish is bought about by a need to follow the path we planned or that society expects us to follow. The job we wanted, the child we needed, the skills we hoped to master, the money we expected to get. However, as we work towards our goals, the gift can so often be that plan completely falling apart. We just don't realise it at the time.

Coming out of London I was mostly on the canal path right through to Windsor. I was trying to navigate getting around a section that had been closed when I met a long haired, thin chap on a Brompton bike who happened to be doing the same. Jason was his name, and he turned out to be ace company for the afternoon. We nattered and navigated our way over to Windsor, maybe 30 miles or more. He waited patiently whilst I did a Heart Radio interview and gallantly carried the ElliptiGO over a couple of styles for me.

We ate a late lunch at an Italian restaurant in Windsor before heading off in different directions. Jason had been full of interest and described the meeting as "such a joy and inspiration, something quite unexpected for my day than I had planned. Thank you for a day I will always remember as a sunny day."

Chance meetings aside, I started to realise it was taking me 10-12 hours to complete my daily mileage. While this was sustainable in the summer months it would not be possible as the days got shorter. I needed to up my game and the pressure to perform better was on; an expectation which plagues us all.

People wonder why I chose to complete this challenge on an ElliptiGO, but the message of kindness and the conversation surrounding it always took precedence and using something as unusual as the ElliptiGO had the potential to raise awareness through the media. It was that simple. ElliptiGO has a whole community of 'Goers', a dedicated and considerate group who love the machine. Any time I put out a post, hundreds of positive interactions would materialise. Most were from America, but when I posted about the challenge, Dan had popped up saying he was always looking for fellow ElliptiGO riders here in the UK. He lived near Oxford with his wife Zoe and offered to join me for two days of riding near Reading.

Having Dan's company was a game changer. I had a pacer, someone to push me to keep going instead of wanting to stop. He was a go-getting, 'yes' person and he and his wife were what you would define as the perfect couple, both beautiful but also really lovely people.

Libby, the support driver, found a free place to park the van – a shack with showers in the corner of a field. She suggested we head to the gravel to park up for the night as heavy rain was forecast. I was happy to follow her direction. A considered and calm personality, she always carefully thought through her choices and reactions.

The following early hours of the morning, a crack of lightning woke me into full consciousness. When a storm arrives in the summer, it starts with the rain. This tiny pattering that you barely even notice. A slightly cool breeze lifts through the heat. The temperature cools just a touch. Then, the rain comes straight down with no veer off in any direction. The rain always appears so much heavier than in the colder months. Suddenly, the ground is flooded – it sneaks up on you.

The rain after the scorching heat is one of my favourite natural phenomena. However, the rain was beating against the window and lightning flashes lit up the van before I had time to even open my eyes. The rain had turned into a storm and Libby was worried about the raised roof of the van and felt we should move. The storm was insistent and demanding, it wanted the world to see it in the darkness. What I found most concerning was Libby was worried that I might think she was overreacting. She was questioning herself because of what I might think or say. Had I become this person, silencing people and dismissing them in a need to 'push on' to the end regardless?

I knew it was not me and not someone I wanted to be, but did I have the time to ask questions of myself and others? Could I be a better leader? I believe I could have, but it would take time away from the situation to really be able to evaluate and consider such things. This was not about being hard on myself, it was about looking in the mirror and saying, how can I be better? How can I be better for people who have given their time to support this mission? I might not get it right, but I needed to forgive myself for that. More importantly I needed to make sure I learned and keep learning, to be better for those around me.

It was 11am and the sky was so dark you could easily have believed that the evening had come early. I saw the storm roll in, the lightening hitting the ground. When I was a child I used to be scared of storms. If I was ever caught out in a storm my mother knew I would be scared and she watched for me out of the window, waiting for me to run down the street to the safety of home. Now I can sit and admire them, feeling nothing but awe. It makes me stop and stare: there is nothing else to do as the sky lights up with every crack of lightening. It was a real test as the rain came down, and it just kept coming. Even my waterproofs stopped working, everything was soaked. My shoes squelched, and streams of water filled my gloved hands.

After Cardiff I made my way to Swansea, but the rain had taken its toll. I popped into The Village Hotel who kindly offered their facilities so I could dry off, have a shower and, as a bonus, use the car park for the support van overnight. Brilliant.

I called my new support driver, who was waiting for me at Swansea Cathedral, and shared the good news. I waited under the canopy of the hotel. I was dripping wet, the cold seeping into my bones but I just kept thinking, *not long now*. I looked out at the rain hitting the ground with force, the grey sky making it seem like evening. A taxi pulled up and Claire, the support driver, clambered out. I knew things were not good despite the gentle smile on her face. It appeared that the support van wouldn't start, which was as you can imagine a major problem. As she spoke, the rain continued to beat down from the all-consuming grey sky.

I guess how the following six hours played out is mostly irrelevant, however what is important is we carried on. We called people, finding a solution. This was not a straight-forward or simple line; it was wiggly and confusing, and we wondered about the choices being made. Eventually my Rotary district leader Tim got hold of a local called Hayley who in turn got hold of a chap called William who ended up fixing the van. From this long line of connections of kindness, we had the van back on the road.

The next day I had to cover 70 miles, my largest day yet. I had to catch up on miles lost, but also complete a tough 3,600ft climb. It was going to be hard, harder than ever. But I knew we would keep going. How we adapt is always our choice, I had learnt this lesson just a few years previously when cycling across America.

# Chapter 6

## Cycling across America: 2018

## "Flying by the seat of your pants."

I flew back home to England from Dubai for the last time in December 2017. The night's warmth hit me as I exited the taxi, piled my suitcases on the trolley and walked into the contrasting coolness of the terminal. I was the first to check in and I upgraded my seat with my airmiles for what I knew might be the last time for a long time. I focused on my breath as I sat in the comfort of the lounge, knowing that my life would look very different next year and forever more.

I watched the sunset through the tiny plane window as the vast desert quickly disappeared into the sea. I laid back. I had no real understanding of what I was about to embark on but at the same time knew I had nothing to lose. My life was undeniably about to change direction and surprisingly the knowing of that did not sit heavily with me, it gave me a sense of hope that maybe I would do something better with myself for the benefit of the world. It has taken me time to understand I do not control my own destiny but that each action I take will propel me towards something wonderful in the end.

When I talked about my plan to cycle 3,000 miles across America, the resistance seemed to double every day. I could hear people suck through their teeth before I had even finished explaining anything about the challenge I was about to undertake. Their doubts swirled in my mind, not quite grabbing hold of me and pulling me to a stop but ensuring that I was constantly questioning myself.

I finished my 15-year career in Facilities Management with my last job in Dubai. I put my house on the market so that I could use the funds for the challenge, and I set off back to the UK in time for Christmas.

I had 10 weeks until I planned to leave. I didn't have a bike, the house still had to sell to fund the trip and, you may see a theme here, I'd done no training. By the time I got around to searching Gumtree for a bike, four weeks had already flown by. I was not, by any stretch of the imagination, a bike expert. So, when selecting which second-hand bike to buy, I chose it based on what it looked like, if it was close-by, and if I got a good feeling from it. I had, believe it or not, done a little research but seemed to have failed to pick up the difference between 'road bikes' and 'touring bikes'.

It didn't seem to be that important because for me this was not about the challenge; I didn't want to develop my personal strength, nor did I have a love of cycling or a lifelong dream waiting to be fulfilled. The reason I was embarking on these challenges was to start a conversation about kindness. So, my time went into planning, trying to get people interested in the story and the idea that kindness and connection has more value than money and our need to focus on it is outdated.

(Well, that's my excuse, and I am sticking to it!)

Christmas arrived far too quickly. The bareness of the trees and the dullness of the landscape did nothing to quell the bite in the air. I spent the festive season at my parents' home, the familiar open fire and delicious home cooked meals providing a welcome retreat. It was the grounding I needed to help the transition from my jet-set lifestyle and mentally prepare myself for a challenge I was unsure was possible for someone like me.

I decided I needed to film the adventure so I could make short videos to share with Sunshine People followers. I specifically wanted a drone so I could get the footage I needed as it followed me across the various and vast landscapes.

"I know a guy who runs a drone film company," said a friend of the family at a Christmas get together. "I can get in touch with him, ask him if he knows a way to get a drone sponsored or give you some hints and tips."

And, just like that, I set off in a new direction. Chatting to this person or that person is how any new idea begins. The offer of some information or a helping hand means we can continue to grow and evolve. It is that simple.

The 'drone guy' turned out to be James, a young self-taught drone operator who had been obsessed with drones for most of his adult life. After a few phone calls to see if I could get a drone donated from a company he knew, James offered to come along and film it himself with expenses paid. Excellent.

His drone skills, as I was to discover, were brilliant, but his addition to the plan presented many other challenges. I needed to ensure that a vehicle, flights, and other additional items were available, and I needed to fund it with the money that was reliant on the sale of my house. So, while it was an absolute gift to have someone to manage filming, it was also a pressure to make it all happen with the additional resources that would be required. As well as this I needed to gain media support, complete route planning, find places to stay and 'train', all in just six weeks.

Three years previously, back in 2015, I made the decision to give up the dream cottage by the sea that myself and Paul had rented together. After his death, I had stayed there for three years on my own and while I had grown so much, his clothes still stayed exactly where he had left them... The superman t-shirt and blue denim jeans at the end of the bed. I couldn't bear to move them.

I knew I had to leave the cottage; I had ultimately been living with a ghost. I could feel him there and, while I was alive, I was not really living. I packed up the house and decided that I would take a trip around the world before settling back in my hometown. I was going to miss the beach, the sun sets, and the hope that Paul might walk back in the front door one day.

I travelled to America first. Leaving the UK felt freeing. I hadn't realised quite how much I had been holding my breath waiting for my life to start again. I had settled down into a seat on the plane, feeling the excitement of travel and freedom while watching the familiar sights of the landing crew making their final checks. Everyone settled down into their own comfortable space. There was a man to my right. He had grey hair, neat looking and sophisticated.

We ended up chatting about life – he had recently retired and so had a lifetime of interesting stories. He talked about his daughters with deep love and affection and told me about his retirement plans with his new partner. I shared the places I planned to visit on my trip. It felt as though I might just find a part of myself that had also died. I could be near the sea, and maybe I could find a new place to breathe for a while. The chap was full of advice, telling me about all of the small towns off the beaten track that I should visit. "You must stop in a small town called Cambria. You will find a restaurant called Lynn's Easy as Pie. It's worth the drive, trust me. Also, a farmers market a little further up…" I scrambled in my bag for pen and paper. "Oh, hang on, let me just write these down."

My flight partner's advice came good. Following the Sat Nav to Cambria was beautiful and as I entered the town, I felt if I blinked, I might miss it. It was flat and low lying like many small towns in America, but it was also homely with a sense of community to entice tourists.

I located somewhere to eat, a small, quaint building drawing my curiosity. It wasn't the restaurant I had been told to visit, but I felt like it was the place I needed to go. I walked in through the glass door. The green wood cladding and glass display counter gave it a cosy feeling. I made my choice from the menu on the back wall. It all looked delicious and I stood there blending in with my white hoodie adorned with the bright Sunshine People logo.

I was greeted by a friendly face. "Hey, how are ya, what can I get ya?" asked the young man behind the counter. He was wearing a large name tag that read 'Daniel'. I perused the board, and, in the end, I chose a panini. "That's a very happy top," said Daniel. I smiled. "Thank you." I looked down at the logo and proceeded to share the story of Sunshine People. After listening intently, Daniel shared his own story.

Daniel's friend had died through suicide just a few years ago. His friend had been a beekeeper and a dearly loved soul. He had battled depression and in the end the depression had won. When Daniel went to the funeral, he decided to make something for the other mourners to take away with them. He made small bees out of black and yellow ropes and gifted them to everyone at the funeral to remind them of their friend, but also to remind them to 'Bee Happy'. He had since gifted over 250 handmade bees across the world.

Fast forward to February 2018, one month before I was due to cycle across America and still without a support vehicle, Daniel put me in touch with a friend who gave me a van to rent.

When we arrived in San Diego to start the two-month, 3,000-mile cycle across America I set off to collect the van. Boarding the train which took me up the Californian coast, I wasn't quite aware of what lay ahead of me. As the train sped past blue skies and the even bluer sea I thought, *how hard can it be?* The journey was calming and in truth I didn't want it to end. Picking up the van would be another step closer to starting and I didn't want to have to get on the bike.

The morning I was due to start cycling I woke up sick. Really sick. I knew I had to get going, but I was not prepared in any way mentally or physically. I had not put in the work needed to build a strong mindset and was flying by the seat of my pants.

Morning turned to afternoon and because of my sickness and some technical difficulties rendering the first film we still hadn't set off. This was not a great start, but it was what it was, and nothing could be done. After endless medication and growing anxiety, we could wait no longer. I set off to the official start point of the San Diego seafront. I had the breakdown of how much distance needed to be covered each day and the late start meant I was behind before I'd even started. The depressing thought did nothing to fuel my mindset. I knew those hills were coming, which also didn't help. What did help was my upbringing, the 'just get on with it' attitude that at times had hindered my emotional intelligence but was going to serve me well. So, I set off. I attempted to get as far as I could.

That day and the next few days were brutal, the hills rolling up out of San Diego relentless. When I saw James and the van at the end of each day, I stopped, climbed in the back and immediately slept. I knew this was the worst part of the trip so if I could get this first week done then that would count as my training. There was very little point in considering the

3,000 miles I had ahead of me, I just had to think of each single day, do as much as I could and see what happened. When a single day seemed too daunting, I broke the mileage down into chunks. I just focused on getting to the next town or landmark, knowing I could then stop and see how I felt.

I knew the roads were pretty sparse in terms of life, a fact that had been confirmed by our first host back in San Diego. What I was not prepared for was the head winds, the like of which I'd never seen before or since. The day the headwinds came, I was on a road with little to no hard shoulder. We pulled over to the side of the road for the night knowing we needed to get to a town 60 miles away for the next stop. As I set off, I realised I was fighting a force of nature. The wind was forcing me backwards. When I peddled the resistance was equal to heading up a 60% gradient, but with an invisible rope pulling me backwards. I was going at about 4mph and even that was extremely hard work. I quickly learnt it was easier to walk but knew I couldn't make the 60 miles like that.

James tried to help by driving the van in front of me for a few miles, acting as a wind break, but it wasn't enough. The road was long and straight with rolling hills. Juggernauts passed by at 70mph and I knew that I was in extreme danger. I had lights and a high vis but if I didn't figure something out then I was at risk of becoming just another white painted bike on the side of the road.

I started to walk on the dirt that ran beside the main road. It was rocky and dusty and not sustainable, but I needed the time to think through my options.

# Chapter 7

## ElliptiGO World Record challenge: 2020

## "Fuel for the soul."

A few years later, as I sat outside an old school friend's house on a wooden dining chair, the heat rising from a fresh cup of tea. I felt comforted by the familiarity. I'd travelled 1,078 miles – one fifth of the required amount to make the World Record and ridden through 20 of the 69 cities.

My body was not as tired as it had been during the first 500 miles. I was getting more used to the general discomfort of the road, becoming numb to it. Today, as I sat with my hair washed and brushed straight down my back, I felt safe. It was my first haircut in nine months, because hairdressers had closed due to COVID. I mentioned this in passing after arriving to stay the night at my friends' home in Buckinghamshire, and she offered to give it a cut.

Rachel, my friend, is like my parents – she's the sort of person who doesn't fuss. She just gets things done and helps people in whatever way she can. It creates a feeling of safety. We tend to fall into what we know; it brings comfort when we need it. I could feel that through these challenges I was discovering what I needed, not only for myself, but also for the people in my life. This was turning out to be an incredible gift in itself.

After the haircut, Rachel and I ate dinner together and I briefly forgot all that I had to do, all the miles that lay ahead. My discomfort at the size of the challenge faded. Good company and a safe place to sleep was having a miracle effect.

I continued my journey the next day. The weather was mild and every mile that went by felt a little better. Cycling was certainly easier now I had new routes that took me off the gravelly cycle paths. I took the half-full attitude; I was one fifth of the way through and soon I would be nearly halfway.

The sun shone as I rode through Welwyn Garden City and I realised I was in a familiar place. Back in the spring of 2011, before all of this, I had taken a new job. The role was not in my field of expertise, but I thought a change of scenery would be good. The town, Ware, was where I had moved to. Then I started dating Paul. My mind was taken back to walks along the canal, sitting in a white lace dress with the sun on my face, a drink in hand and love in my heart. I passed by the Greek restaurant we had eaten in, walking back hand in hand in the dappled moonlight after an evening of excess.

This place reminded me of dating Paul and what unconditional love felt like. He would call me every day and visit as much as he could, as I did with him. However, we had been five hours drive from each other and his emails became more and more focused on how we might spend every day together. Those first three months had been filled with longing and a deep passion. The memories fell upon me like rain as I rode through the sunshine.

Riding through the town brought back so many overwhelming feelings. I wanted to stop at our favourite bar on the canal and sit and have a drink, imagine him sitting with me, teasing me fondly. But I still had miles to go, so I chose instead to take all of these feelings and use them to propel me to my final destination.

The morning of the 26th August, I'd been on the road for 26 days and the whole challenge had changed shape. I'd travelled 1,238 miles travelled, zig-zagging my way up the country. I wanted to spend my time cycling around

Cambridge; the flat roads, the cycle paths, the beautiful old stone buildings and historic atmosphere. However, I had a place to be, and that place was Leamington Spa. It was a 75-mile day, tough but not impossible.

Buckinghamshire and Northamptonshire passed by; the headwind strong. I felt myself wavering. On the outskirts of Northampton, I stopped and picked some wild blackberries, wondering if the energetic figurative wall I had been avoiding had finally found me.

Suddenly, I feel a series of chills and an all-encompassing need to sleep. I curled up and closed my eyes on a wicker two-seater chair outside of a park café. I don't think I slept but my body shut down for a while. *This is enough, you've had enough.*

I ignored the little voice of doubt and went into the café. I ordered some food, ate, and took a minute to consider my options. The headwind had been brutal. What felt like 100 miles was in fact only 55. I wanted to believe I could complete the final 20, but I didn't have it in me.

The cafe was closing and so I sat outside on the tarmac, with my back against the wall. I looked across at the bright green grass and with no other option I called a contact, Steve, at the Hilton Hotel, who arranged for me to spend a night at the Northampton branch. It was such a great help, but I wasn't sure if I even had it in me to ride the three miles to get to the hotel.

Those three miles were hell. I felt like I would never get there. Just three short miles. In that moment, they were the hardest of the ride so far.

When I arrived I couldn't help but cry. I was internally on my knees, physically and mentally exhausted, but more than that I was grateful. Yes, I was powering the bike, but it was the people who were powering me. The generosity, the kind conversations, the problem solving. This was not my ride, it was everyone's.

A few days previously, I left Stanstead at the crack of dawn to avoid the rain. I gave it everything I had, feeling a little unsafe on some roads and unsure if I should be on them. I kept pushing on. By 24 miles in, I was drenched. The rain had not heard the weather forecast and decided to come uninvited. Fear and rain made me ready to stop, so when up popped a bright yellow neon McDonalds 'M', it was a glorious sight.

After pancakes and a hot chocolate, I stood outside under the awning that spanned the length of the building, getting myself ready to face the rain again. A woman wandered up to me with curiosity and asked, "Are you going far?"

I was going far. I explained briefly what I was doing and before I had finished, she smiled broadly. "Oh yes, I saw you on the BBC, oh brilliant, I am so glad I got to see you," she said. It was a tiny moment, but it felt important. The message was out there. This woman, who had recognised me on the side of the road outside a fast-food restaurant, had heard the story. It had impacted her, and she was inspired to be kinder because of it.

I had felt irritated by myself, the rain and everything that was going on, but the recognition brought a lightness to my demeanour. I felt myself soften. It was moments like this that brought the sunshine in the rain.

Riding the ElliptiGO gave me time to think, so much time! While on the road from Cambridge I started thinking about the types of people there are in the world. I know there are hundreds of types of people with varying personalities, but I was starting to see that during this challenge, the people I met fell into two main categories. One, the fearful, and two, the fearless. The yes and no folks. Those who take control and those who let life control them. The owners and the blame shifters. I had seen these two categories of people present themselves throughout all of my challenges. Could you really live your life to the fullest when living in darkness, unprepared and unwilling to lift your head out of the sand? After pondering this for an hour or so, my conclusion was simply this: we all need to embrace life because it's so short, too short.

I pushed passed the physical pain and mental anguish, finally making it to the stunning cathedral in Ely. At this point, I'd racked up total of 1,450 miles. I could feel the wind in my bones as I captured an obligatory selfie in front of the majestic building. There was something in me that was growing, a seed that felt like loneliness that if watered would grow into something much bigger. I decided to stop earlier and sought out a place to stay, needing to recuperate.

I had a few hours to kill, so with a chill seeping through my core, I went to find a warm place to send some emails. I gently rode the bike down the back streets before I found a place with big windows and glass double doors. Checking it over to see if Charis could come in with me, the smell of comfort food wafted out of a kitchen somewhere out of sight. To the left of the entrance there were a number of high stools and even higher tables. I plonked myself down in the only free space, took off my helmet and ordered. The other tables were occupied by a smiley, middle-aged man with an interest in Charis, and another with a middle-aged couple passing the time quietly. We started to talk between the three tables.

As so often is the case in these chance conversations with strangers, I found myself opening up to them. Reassured by my honesty, they began to share their stories with me.

The woman in the couple told me she was HIV positive and had been in an abusive relationship. Her new partner appeared to be quiet and unassuming. He listened but he didn't engage.

"I know what kindness is," she said. "I know what it is because I have experienced so much unkindness. It's not that I need sympathy, but you know, you just sometimes learn from all the bad that happens."

She asked me about my project, and we continued to talk about life and kindness. As she left, she handed me some money towards my night's accommodation and gifted me food from her own shopping bag that she was just taking home. I said it was ok, but she insisted. I didn't know her situation, but I got the impression she wasn't a millionaire. But what she had; she was prepared to give if someone else needed it. It struck me hard, deep in my soul, and I found it hard not to cry with gratitude. It's often what happens when people are kind to me.

The chap sat at the other table was a jovial man called Pete. He asked me about the bike and what I was doing with genuine interest. Then he asked a question that I will never forget.

"When was the last time you were told you were enough?" I looked at him and didn't say anything. I let his words sink in. Eventually, I said, "I'm not sure I have. But then… Maybe I don't need to be told."

We went on to talk about Pete's recent suicide attempt, and his children. He was, on occasion emotional, but was clear minded and talked as though he was sharing what needed to be shared.

"I've met nice people and I've also met arseholes from every country in the world. You are not allowed to acknowledge an arsehole is an arsehole," he said. I sat and listened, enjoying his thoughts and his company. He was smart, original and didn't run with the crowd. I don't know if he will manage to move through the suicidal thoughts or if the short time I spent with him made a difference. I hope it does.

The next day, I continued back on the bike. The landscape was largely flat. I mean, there were some hills, but in comparison to what I had been through it might as well have been the Great Plains of America. Some find flat land boring, but I enjoy the vastness. I like being able to see the horizon at the furthest point possible. Maybe that's why I love the sea so much. To see the world fall away is a wonderful reminder of possibility, and also how tiny we really are.

I pootled along tarmacked, single-track farm roads that ran between fields, a cyclist's dream. I was then stopped by a chap in a truck.

"What brings you this way then?" He asked, with a certain air about him that made me feel like maybe I was trespassing. There was a sizing up of the situation that happened in a split second: I smiled at him. The universal language. "My navigation bought me this way."

"So, what's this?" He pointed to the bike. I went on to explain why and what I was riding Charis for. He got out of the truck and came around to me. He asked me more questions than anyone else had yet with genuine interest; how many cities, how had the cities been decided, what defined a city, how far had I gone, how far would I go? At the end he said, "Bless ya. An' you watch out for the hills, won't you." I was on my way again down straight endless roads through the flat fields.

As I carried on, the wind was sometimes against me and sometimes it was not. I was loving the ride but wanted it to be finished in equal measure. I watched the fluffy dandelion seeds, nature's fairies, floating in the air. With no intention other than existence and no thought for past or future, they were a reminder that I needed to tune in to the here and now.

My day off in Norwich was restful for the most part but I had also managed to get Charis fixed while I was there. As I left the city and the much-needed break, I planned to do a 91-mile day – my longest so far. As I hit the flats 20 miles out of Norwich the headwinds were pushing me back. Given the choice between hills or flats with a headwind, I'd choose hills any day of the week. The flats seemed endless. Something sunk from me, there was a physical change in my psyche in that moment as my belief failed me. It was caught on the wind and carried away by the breeze.

I'd envisaged myself scooting along at 16 mph completing the 91 miles with great ease. That dream was quickly squashed, and I was working twice as hard to get half as far. It was heart breaking, and while that might sound dramatic, when the distance is all you have and all you focus on, day in day out, this is the only way to describe it.

The lack of hills or protection on the flat land meant the headwind doubled down and kept me working hard for most of the ride. There was no respite, but I had no other options. I had to get where I needed to go. I didn't stop. I knew I had no time and I was losing light quickly. The idea that I might not get there until after dark made me uneasy.

There was a fine rain coming down, the type you barely notice as it drenches you. I had just one more hour until the light faded. As I came to the end of a shopping precinct I bore right under an arch and Peterborough Cathedral presented itself in all its glory. It was the most majestic cathedral I had seen to date. I wanted to stay, to go around and feel the energy of the place. It was beautiful in the rain and I imagined it would be even more stunning on a sunny day. I took myself to an imaginary place where I was lying on the grass in the sunshine with nothing to do but watch the people go by, the majestic building towering above me, silently sharing stories of the unknown. My mind wanted me to stop, to keep me safe, but I continued to pedal.

I had managed to get back across to the other side of the country. I was 1,765 miles in and powering onwards towards Liverpool and my next planned day off. I would have to tackle the North Wales coastline first to make it across to Bangor. I felt like it had the potential to be a dream, skirting the edge of the countryside and the beaches I loved so much. Today, however, I was due to set off at 8am. I seriously struggled with the idea of pedalling 67-miles. The plan had been to head to Derby, then Stoke-on-Trent, and then on to stay at my next host's house for the evening. The host, Claire, lived 15 miles the other side of Stoke-on-Trent. It was too much, and I knew it.

However, there was a clear voice in my head, telling me, "Well, that was the plan, you need to stick to the plan." The deep feeling in my gut that hinted at failure. I have learnt that following the first plan does not always work out for the best. There is something in us that wants to tell us we're a failure even when we haven't failed yet. We spend so long beating ourselves up for not doing every task that we set ourselves. We are our own worst critics, but sometimes we need to relent and say, *it's ok to give myself a break. I won't do it every day, just when I need to, so that I can carry on to the big end goal without burning out.*

So, with this in mind, I took Derby out of the equation; I knew I would be passing through it on the way back down when I spelt out the word 'kindness' on my Strava map.

Skipping Derby meant that the day was just 43 miles, but the 'faffing and planning' time vortex that I often found myself in, meant I left an hour late. The day started with hills, up and down in quick succession, and the miles were tough. The first 10 miles of any day were always the worst.

Stoke-on-Trent is a city without a cathedral. I found this disappointing and wondered if a firmly worded letter might remedy this. I was enjoying my cathedrals – they were all completely unique and breath taking.

Just seven miles before my final destination the rain came again. It was like nothing I had ever seen in the UK. I abandoned Charis on the roadside and ran to a bus stop to shelter from the downpour. In just10 minutes, the roads had turned to rivers. The only storm I had seen that was similar was in Vietnam, when I was teaching English as a foreign language on a three-month working holiday. Vietnam was tough and humbling and, as usual, I felt as if I wasn't good enough. But when I wasn't teaching, I used the time to write my first book while enjoying the power of a simpler life. Back then, I was at the desk in my room on my day off, writing and passing the time. When I heard the storm break, it felt as if the sky was coming down to crush us all. The explosion of thunder sounded as if it were right outside my window. The deafening cracks were quickly followed by torrential rain. Within a few minutes the streets were flooded as the people below ran for cover and little motorised 'tuc tucs' rode faster through the streets to safety.

When I got back to Charis, sodden and fed up, I apologised for leaving her and continued on to Claire's house.

Soon after arriving on the sloped hill of Claire's drive, I was greeted by a smiling and welcoming face. I stepped up into the porch, heaved Charis into the hallway and immediately felt at home. A cup of tea was made, and an introductory chit chat was had from the comfort of the living room. Claire soon went off to pick up her son, and told me to help myself to anything, get a shower or bath and such like. An immediate trust was bestowed upon me, giving me a sense of safety. As I popped back down the stairs after putting all of my equipment on charge, I peeked into the snack box she had left for me. I stood with my back to the kitchen units and munched through a packet of mini cookies, taking a breath. The heaviness I carried left me and was replaced by a sense of comfort and wellbeing.

I wandered back upstairs. Claire's son had given up his room to me and so, surrounded with Star Wars and the cosiness of childhood dreams, I settled down to rest for an hour.

Claire returned and came upstairs to tell me dinner was ready. "Would you like stuffing?" she asked. As we laughed, she followed up with "...yes, you've come to *that* house... And while we're at it, leg or breast?" We laughed at our similar humour and I went downstairs a few minutes later to find a large stuffing and breast awaiting me on a plate.

I liked Claire a lot. She fed me enough to fill me up (quite some feat), bantered and laughed, and most of all she was kind. I hope our paths cross again. The people I met really were the best part of the gruelling relentlessness. Much like cycling across America, we are fuelled by the souls of good people.

# Chapter 8

## Cycling across America: 2018

## "From failure to success and back again."

Skip back to my cycle across America in 2018, and I was experiencing much the same challenges.

On one particular day, I had been pushing against the headwind for a few hours and managed to cover the grand total of five miles. It felt as if my soul was leaving my body. The distance I had to cover was swirling in my mind. The juggernauts whizzing by so fast on the long, straight road nearly toppled me over, heightening my fear. I was just 10 days into the 58 it would take me to reach the other side of America. Everything felt so far away. I looked across the land, at the mild colours of what nothing in particular looks like. Shrubs that were a murky shade of green blended into the brown landscape. In the distance, the landscape changed to hills. The contrast was like something in a painting.

I looked out at it all and considered what I might do to lessen the fear. I took a breath. How could I reduce the risks but go faster than walking? I was pondering this when my phone rang, disturbing my thoughts. I picked up.

"Hello, is that Nahla? It's the Silver City Press. I wondered if now would be a good time to talk about the story we want to run on you?"

Now was absolutely the perfect time. I needed to move my thoughts onto something other than the overwhelming feelings of inadequacy. The whispers on the breeze continued to tell me that I was not good enough. I needed to let these words be blown away. As I talked about what I was doing and more importantly why, something shifted.

"That's really great," said the reporter. "So, just explain, why do you not ask for money, and ask people to be kind to others instead?"

It was an answer I'd given many times, and I replied without a moment's hesitation. "We measure so much of our success on money, but when the end of our lives come, none of that will matter. You will only remember the relationships you had, the things you did for others, the impact you had and the impact others had on you. As I said, I met a stranger on a beach whose kindness was a catalyst for me living my life. There is story upon story out there that shares a similar tale... Meetings that have transformed people's lives, a moment of kindness, a moment of human connection. That is something that no amount of money can buy."

"Brilliant," said the reporter. "So, you mention that social media is really important in your quest. Why is that?"

"Social media is not going anywhere, and neither is our media," I said. "Ok, let me give you an example. When you want to get physically fit, what do you do?"

"I go to the gym." The reporter responded

"Yes, and you'd probably look at everything you ate too right?" I said.

"Yes," the reporter agreed. "So, your brain is a muscle also, and what we feed it is not just what we eat but also everything we see. Every story we read, every video we watch. It's like going to gym for your brain."

I went on to explain that when we focus on watching things that inspire us, we will be inspired. If we watch people shooting each other we will tend to feel sad or bad about that. Our brains copy and follow what we see in social media. We are pack creatures and so generally follow a crowd, in one form or another. Following kindness stories and promoting them only supports and creates a stronger, brighter society.

"It feeds peoples' brains and gives them the workout they need for a healthy mindset and overall wellbeing," I finished.

After I got off the phone, the wind died down and like magic the voices on the breeze were quiet. My energy was recharged, and I felt ready to face whatever the road had to give me. I got on the tarmac and pedalled as if nothing else in the world mattered. I needed to get to the end, to push on through. I was determined now. I kept vigilant; listening out for trucks and jumping off the road when necessary. I pedalled through the pain, the doubt, and the exhaustion, because thanks to a well-timed phone call I was reminded that what I was doing was not about me, it was about the message which we all needed to hear (including me) that kindness is king. The rolling hills meant that the trucks could not see me and so when I pedalled into the final stop for the day it was with great relief. Even so, I knew the vast desert was next, and this gave me a sense of unease.

The next day, when I made my way through the desert's sloping, sweeping dunes of yellow sand, shapes and shadows constantly distorted by the passing winds, the weather was getting warmer. I wanted to stop and take in the spectacular views but there was no time. I had to keep to the schedule. As I would discover, the desert I'd been so worried about would become one of my favourite parts of the journey.

Unlike the UK, America has huge swaths of land filled with not a whole lot. You can cycle for a day and not see anything except sporadic fast-food restaurants. Takeaways and unhealthy food joints gather together around the entrances and exits to even the tiniest of towns. It was both comforting and shocking. I spent the day rolling through the largely uninhabited sandy desert wondering when a place to rest might appear as a mirage on the horizon. It was nearing the end of the day when at last, a large old wooden shack that doubled up a go kart track and small café came into sight. It was all closed up with some people sat outside at picnic benches. I pulled up.

To my surprise, there were also two cyclists taking some rest. Their bikes, mounted up with camping gear, told me they were also heading across America. "Hey, is it all shut up here?" I asked as I unclipped my helmet. "Yeah, just a little while ago," one of the cyclists, a lady, said. "So, where are you heading?" I asked. "Heading across America ending in St Augustine." "Cool, me too," I said. We shared stories about why we were making our journeys. The cyclists told me they thought they had camped not far from me further back along the journey, on the day where the headwinds had been particularly bad. It gave me hope to see and talk with fellow cyclists, and a reminder that so often we're on the same journey as others despite believing we're alone. I had felt so isolated until then, but now there were two people trying to achieve the same goal as me. I thought, well, if these real people that I can touch and see can achieve this, then maybe it wasn't going to be so bad after all.

Every state in America has their own rules, so fortunately for me in some states I could ride the highways. It seems odd to be grateful for this but being on relatively flat roads with a wide hard shoulder was a true gift. The road surfaces left much to be desired, but I took what I could get. My first highway trip nearly killed me, the jarring up my legs, my arms (and mostly my arse!) was like someone had beaten me within an inch of my life. To numb the pain, I used an interesting form of mindfulness. The sides of highways were full of the most unusual things. The biggest tyres known to man, a hammer, a doll, some unidentified roadkill (not because it was too mangled, but because I'd never seen that animal before), a couple of snakes and what looked like a kitchen cooker. I focused on each new oddity like it was a prize on the Generation Game. In a weird way, it kept me going, distracting me from my ailments.

Eventually it was time to leave the highway. I cycled up the sloping junction and turned left. What lay ahead of me was a long, straight road out into the barren and hot land of the unknown. Barely any traffic had followed me and there was a hard shoulder that was adequate in size but not necessarily in surface. The slight slope of the road allowed me to glide for a bit, and I saw the black support van ahead of me. James, the driver, had not been able to complete any filming on the highway and so had found the first safe spot to park for the day. Sometimes, when you're pushing yourself to your limits, it's not until you stop that you realise how much pain you're enduring. I laid down on a mat with the bike dumped beside me and rocked on my back to bring some normality to my failing body.

One week in, and I was getting use to the riding. I mean it didn't stop me from moaning incessantly about it, the constant aches and friction burns. I kept asking myself, "What the hell am I doing?" As always, I accepted I was on the road and just had to just keep going.

I crossed paths with a group of around 10 middle aged men on bikes, bumping into them several times over the next few days. They were making their way across America too. They were jovial and cheeky and behaved at least 20 years their junior. I had stopped for a minute on a long straight road with a wide hard shoulder. Suddenly, two of the guys were by my side. The sun had been shining for most of the day and as one took off his sunglasses the whites around his eyes confirmed this fact. "How are you doing?" asked one of the men. "Yeah, I'm ok," I said.

"I was just taking a stop. Where are your group?" "Oh, some are behind, some up ahead," said the other. "We heard you squeaking past us earlier. Do you want some oiling?"

My eyebrows raised. "You know, your chain there. Have you got oil?" he said. "Ah, no. I don't."

With that he went about oiling my chain. I hadn't even known it needed to be done, but to save face I thought I'd leave that tiny fact out.

Somewhere around day 15, the route led me through more 'nothingness', vast swaths of land with beauty in its emptiness. Up ahead I could see a cyclist had stopped. I hoped it would be one of my friends-on-the-road, Tracy, and luckily for me as I got closer, I saw that it was. She was fast becoming my go-to person as we repeatedly crossed each other's paths. Her partner Martin had left to head home and so she was alone too. While the landscape had changed, the road was long and quiet. Cacti scattered the land for as far as I could see. Rock faces emerged at times to cloud my view to the edge of the earth.

The silence on the roads was equally eerie and encouraging. I was to discover it was because this road had been replaced by a main highway. However, it allowed time for Tracy and I to safely stop on the hard shoulder and compare stories from the routes we had travelled. We were both heading to the same place, a small town called Duncan. We set off and said we would meet there.

I was already optimistic, revelling in the fact that I was a quarter of the way through the ride. As I rode along, the wind swirled, the sun shone and traffic including large juggernauts started to appear in both directions. There some hard shoulder to work with but, as anyone who has a juggernaut pass them on a bike will know, a hard shoulder is no consolation, but I told myself, it's better than no hard shoulder at all.

As I rode on, the wind started to pick up even more. The dust swirled into my face and a growing sense of unease rose in my body as I kept pedalling rhythmically to propel myself forwards. I could hear the trucks increase in noise, see them take over my vision and feel the air batter me as they passed by. After a while, as the traffic got heavier, the road took a large sweeping direction to the left. It opened up to a large downhill slope. I could see the landscape in its totality, and the long road leading me down into the town of Duncan. I had just a couple of miles to go if that, but the wind was so strong I had to keep the brakes on. Eventually, I had to get off and walk. The road was now jammed with vehicles, slowly creeping to a standstill. A police car weaved through the traffic and pulled up next to me.

"Where you headed?" asked the police officer, rolling down the window and studying me. "I'm trying to get to Duncan. I think that's it." I pointed down the mile to the bottom of the hill. "It's too dangerous for you to be on here," said the officer. "There's a sandstorm coming, so we've had to pull everyone off the highway. That's why the road is so busy. You won't be able to travel anymore. Let's get your bike in the back."

I soon updated my social media accounts, letting everyone know I'd had to stop because of the storm, saying thanks to the officer and hopefully warning others on the same route. After reading comments later that day, it turned out that the officer was someone quite high up in the ranks. I just thought he was a superhero.

I'd previously discovered that the group of 10 guys had been whittled down to three. Some had given up and some had headed home to be adults again. So, arriving in Duncan, I saw the three musketeers had set up camp in the local park. I sat with them a while and accepted a beer. We sat around and chatted about the storm and what our plans were. The town seemed protected, and unaffected in the most part. It looked like one of the musketeers wasn't going to make it all the way to St Augustine as he had planned, he was already talking about giving up. With that comparison, I was wondering if I might be a little stronger than I thought. The men were really just boys enjoying the ride, which I had a lot of respect for. Over our beers, we decided to meet up later that evening to eat together. Tracy was in town too, so I invited her along.

Tracy was staying at the town's only B&B and it just so happened they also had Warm Showers guest accommodation in the back garden. This took the form of a tin shepherds' hut, which worked just fine for me. The hosts were also happy to allow us to put the van in the back yard with their equally sweet (if not a little mad) goats.

The restaurant was also the only one in town, but its menu was vast and was good enough to feed us all. It was a typical American diner with booths and served the classic all-American breakfast I had grown to enjoy a little too much. Next door was a shop, sparse and a little odd, connected to the restaurant by a little alcove. There was a gentle quietness around the table as we sat together, not awkward but a sign of mutual exhaustion and simply enjoying the feeling of safety that was so distant on the road. There is something important about eating together, breaking bread and sharing the moment. It connects us on a deeper level. I miss the tradition of sitting around the table to eat, which, in my opinion, is very underestimated in its power to resolve the world's problems.

At this point, my stomach had started to cause me some real issues. I was going to the toilet five or six times a day and sharing any more detail with you would be too much. The pain was constant. As I was only on day 15, the idea of continuing was giving me serious cause for concern. Little did I know, it was only the start of a long road of health conditions that would plague me as a consequence of the challenges I would undertake.

Once the sandstorm had passed, I cycled on from Duncan, wishing my friends luck and hoping we would meet again.

After spending most of the time in a fight or flight state, I held on to the knowledge that at some point in the future I would feel a little safer. After a few days of almighty lows, today was that day. I was heading through Phoenix and into Queens Valley. The sun was shining, and it felt as if there was hope ahead. I knew from my plan that I had miles of cycle paths to follow. The flat lands and industrial areas filled my vision, stretching all the way to the horizon, and there was something strangely comforting from it. The lack of cars was a considerable factor. The air was thick, enveloping me. Music played in my ear and as I approached a slight slope on the smooth concrete carpet, I saw what appeared to be a rope across the path.

I got a little closer and, fortunately for both of us, quickly realised that it was a huge snake. The legless reptile was sprawled out, enjoying the sun. It was as if the world was conspiring to keep me in a state of fear f-o-r-e-v-e-r! I summarised my options. There was a 20 cm gap between the snake's tail and the edge of the path. However, my guts churned at the thought of passing so closely. Then, up the hill towards me came a cyclist who passed through the gap with no problem whatsoever. Once on my side, he spurred me on and kept an eye out for me as I made my break. I waved and shouted out my thanks to him. I came back to focusing on the surroundings, the sunshine, and the comforting thickness of the air. After a little time, I started to feel calm once again.

Miles and miles of cycle paths ensued and as I carried on out of the industrial lands I moved into the city's suburbs. Following the cycle path carefully with the warm breeze funnelling through me, I kept propelling myself along. For the first time since I'd set off, I felt like I had nowhere in particular to be. I was simply cycling.

The smells changed as I went through each area. As the river ran to my left for the most part, the smell of fresh water gave off a coolness that I appreciated. Pockets of refreshing air would encompass me for a few seconds as I continued to ride. From one side of the city to the next I saw every neighbourhood. Further along the river, the pathway was less well maintained. The roofs were held together with gaffer tape and the odd cable tie. A black American woman shouted out expletives at – from what I gathered – her cheating boyfriend. Boys fished in the river, hopeful for what looked like their next dinner. Shopping complexes and road networks could be seen in the distance as I followed the path, passing over road after road. Potholes as big as my wheels littered the poorer areas, as if someone had conveniently forgotten to log it into the maintenance schedule. The smell of garden BBQs wafted into my path and I listened to the rhythm of the pedals turning and the occasional ting of the bike bell I'd been given by a friend.

I was relaxing, but with that I was feeling the inequality of life like a sledgehammer. It was such a stark contrast to the palatial second homes for the rich that I passed not long after. The neat gardens and security systems. The balconies and glass fronts. The new, neat construction. It smelt of money. What do we do about injustice? What do we do about inequality? I didn't have the answers, but what I knew was that I could feel it deep in my soul that day.

I wasn't going to clock up the mileage I had hoped for that day and had to stop. I travelled up to stay with Debbie and John, my Warm Shower hosts for this leg of the journey. Debbie had recovered from several bouts of cancer and had a calming warmth that put me at ease. The next day Debbie, a cyclist herself, offered to ride with me for 35 miles. We took the easiest route. The ride was the furthest she had done since her recent recovery, but she willingly gave it a go. Her company gave me a new energy for the journey. It was so much easier with her cycling with me. When it was time for us to part ways, I didn't want to leave, and hoped that we'd meet up and hang out again soon.

The day of luxury soon turned into a literal hell. I thought the worst of the hills were over, but I wasn't even close. The roads that followed twisted and wound around the hills, cutting into the inland cliff faces. As I looked ahead of me, the road seemed to climb forever. As I went over a large bridge, all around me were rock formations and sheer drops. The road had been carved to lie between them all. The stony giants towered over me, grey and unforgiving, the drops threatening to take me. Occasional glimpses of the next risky road ahead snuck through the gaps between the rocks. I should have been able to appreciate the scenery, but the brutality of the climb blocked out the landscape's rugged beauty. Tunnels ran through the middle of cliff faces, vast and imposing. The noise of the juggernauts was enough to stop my heart.

I started to realise I might not be able to complete the challenge. An overwhelming feeling came over me. I was not able to physically think or speak, my body shutting down as fear took over. No hard shoulders and a near miss with a truck spiralled me into a place where I found the van, curled up in a ball in the back, and attempted to steady my mind. After some time, I could function again. I got back on the bike. Eventually, after hitting the lowest point of the challenge so far, I subsequently arrived at a place called Top of the World. The irony was not lost on me. I had learnt how quickly a day can change, and how easy it was to go from a mindset of failure to one of strength. Our environments have a huge impact on our mental state, and in this harsh stony world I was laying myself bare on the rocky rollercoaster of life.

I was reminded of this moment as I hit the north of England on the ElliptiGO. What I had learnt was that the rollercoaster doesn't stop, but you learn to ride it a little easier. A tolerance and a resilience builds up... Well, a little bit, anyway.

# Chapter 9

# ElliptiGO World Record challenge: 2020

## "Miracle foot care"

The sun rose from the sea as though it had woken for the first time, the water mirroring the oranges and reds. The promenade drew out to a point in the far distance.

I had not made it very far from my accommodation that morning, but I already wanted to stop and stare. To watch the ripples from the sea rise and fall on the sand in a gentle and calming rhythm. To sit on the edge of the promenade and be reminded of a quieter time, of being loved so deeply I could barely breathe. However, I had to keep going across to Bangor, the most westerly city on the north coast of Wales. I would be back here again on the same day.

On the wide pathway of the promenade sat huge, red, looming 3D letters announcing that I was at 'Colwyn Bay'. Colwyn is pretty beautiful, with an old castle and long sandy beach. It also has the 'smallest house' in Great Britain. Who knew? Well, now you do. If it comes up on a quiz you can thank me later.

I wanted to breathe it all in, the whole view, the sea, the skies. I wanted it to be sucked into my very being because I knew I couldn't stay. I had to keep on going.

During the challenge I was also generating PR opportunities. Coming into the North of England I was hopeful that they might pick up the Free Listening session I'd set up in Liverpool. I was looking forward to the ride back from Bangor, with the wind behind me in the sunshine. I was shattered but it certainly did feel good to be going with the wind this time. Heading back on a road I'd already travelled felt easier. I knew what was to come. It felt familiar, and for the past five weeks everything had been new. The wind and I were at last friends, going along together in harmony.

I always feel great empathy for people who find themselves without somewhere to sleep for the night. For some people, that uneasy feeling is part of daily life. There are many who don't know if they will ever get to sleep in a bed again. So, when I say I had nowhere to stay in North Wales, I do not for one moment believe the situation was as desperate as it could be. I knew, or at least hoped, that something would come up eventually.

I needed somewhere for two nights. Claire, the bright spark I had stayed with earlier on in the trip, had cleverly posted on an online mothers' groups in the area around Colwyn Bay. I received a message back from Helen. She had a spare outhouse with blow up bed. She explained she lived with her husband and two teenage children. She told me she would be back from work at around 5ish and to let her know if I was interested. I jumped at it, of course.

Later that day I arrived at Helen's drive. It was being dug up and renovated. I headed to the large outhouse at the back of the house. I sighed with relief. A roof and some safety were all I really needed. My challenges were showing me how little I actually needed to get by. Basic requirements, food, warmth and the kindness of strangers. Helen invited me to eat with the family and their company was easy and heart-warming.

Staying with Helen was a joy. Meeting people who put their faith and trust in you and getting to experience the good from that is a wonderful thing. We can so often be fearful of being kind, but Helen and her family faced it head on and she said as much. This approach had taught her children how to be kind. I've said it a thousand times – kindness is a gift that keeps on giving in so many ways.

The next day, leaving Colwyn Bay and heading along the North Wales coast to Liverpool, the wind was behind me and the sun shone. It was a wonderful feeling. I kept trying to pull myself back into the moment, to say, "It's ok, I don't need to fill every second, it's ok to take the day a little easier and go with the flow." I enjoyed the sun's reflections on the beach, watching my shadow as I followed the direction of the wind. I wanted to remember it forever, a snapshot in time that no one else will ever see, just a place in my memories.

As I went over the bridge from Wales into Liverpool the sun continued to shine, but the winds got a little hairy to say the least. The unicorn tailwind had spoilt me and now I was pushing to get to 8mph along the flat as I neared my final destination.

The ElliptiGO has to be the greatest conversation starter since the invention of the dog. As I pushed against the winds, the open flat area soon narrowed to a more sheltered cycle path. It was a welcome relief and on my left, I spied a café where many cyclists had stopped to enjoy the balmy September weather. I pulled in. Everyone came to talk to me about Charis and what I was doing. People helped me fix the bike and tighten the chain to give myself a fighting chance against the winds.

A few days later, I was on the next leg of the journey, 37 miles from Liverpool to Manchester along a cycle path running next to the dual carriageway that connected the two cities. As I cycled, I heard a loud horn. I turned to look and saw the driver looking at me. He pointed, winked, and gave me a thumbs up. It made me feel he knew what I was doing and why, that he was giving his approval as he passed, a bit of motivation to keep me going. It stuck with me all day, a feeling that I was alright and accepted, that maybe I was worthy. Someone had seen me and had given their seal of approval. It was a huge gift, and he wouldn't have even realised it.

Arriving at the Manchester Hilton Deansgate was a huge relief. When I walked into my room on the top storey of the hotel, I was greeted with a floor-to-ceiling glass wall that gave me a view of the entire city. The idea of having to move again the next day was daunting, but I'd now broken the back of the ride and would be halfway in just 500 miles (approximately 10 days). It was a great feeling, but I knew the challenging hills of Scotland and the Peak District awaited me.

After eating and completing some admin tasks, I had a rare moment of time to myself. In an attempt to relax before the next stint, I ran a bath. I felt a sense of accomplishment as I sunk into the deep hot water, using the small bottle of complimentary body wash to build a surface of bubbles – a moment of self-made luxury. I felt safe, secure, and ready to take on the road the next day. I picked up the bar of chalk-white hotel soap, revelling in the feeling of being clean after a hard day's ride. And that's when I found it. A large lump in my right breast.

The strangest sense of calmness washed over me as I rinsed off the soap. It was a feeling I'd never experienced before. I stared ahead of me at the shiny taps. Then I got out the bath mechanically. My mind didn't chatter as loudly as usual; whispers of words came but nothing I could put my finger on. I pulled on my clothes and, as usual in these situations, made a cup of tea.

I left the curtains open that night so I could see the city lights. I had a fitful night's sleep and as the dawn broke, I watched the sun slowly illuminate the hills I was due to tackle.

The sun bounced off the city's skyscrapers, the silvery grey buildings contrasting starkly against the blues skies. In a single day, I needed to climb and descend the hills of the Peak District. This knowledge only encouraged the deep sense of foreboding in my gut. I had to continue. This was not the ending to this story; this was not going to be an excuse to quit.

The day before finding the lump in my breast I'd decided to do a Free Listening session when I was in Liverpool, not least of all because I liked how the Ls sounded together. I spent a much-needed day off there, supporting a social initiatives along the way called Urban Confessional, which had been set up by Ben Mathes, an American guy. The idea is that you stand anywhere, holding up a sign with the words 'Free Listening' on it, and people will come and speak to you. Your job is simply to listen without judgement, not to give advice or guidance. I was moved by the idea. There are so many people in the world that do not feel heard. So many of their worries are never spoken about because there's simply no one to hear them.

Liverpool city centre is modern and well put together. To some, it is a country all of its own. Its culture is unique, and the loyalty of its residents is renowned. Standing with a sign in the middle of the pedestrianised shopping area allows you to watch the world go by and wonder about the people in it. The homeless man with odd shoes who looked as if he was only just holding onto life. The girls, immaculately put together, but who had their own inner struggles and insecurities. The people off to work, and those clearly on a holiday. The fearful and the confident. The differences were glaringly obvious. I watched their expressions and heard their conversations as they passed me, a fly on the wall. It was the ex-forces guy looking for work that I'll never forget. I wanted to speak to him but didn't get to before he had moved on; something I will think about a lot over my life no doubt. If I had been in my own world, watching my phone, consumed by my own thoughts and worries, all of it would have passed me by.

A lady wandered up to me and asked what I was doing. She talked and I listened. I heard enough to know that she felt a deep-rooted pain. It is our responsibility, all of us, to try to understand what it is like to stand in the shoes of someone else. An awareness of how others see the world is key to our ability to co-exist and, more than that, to be kind.

I had made it over to the other side of the country, Darlington area, however I knew the day was going to be brutal due to the pain in my foot. By the time I'd pedalled about 40 miles the pain was all consuming and when I had to stop at a junction it was excruciating to push off again. I stopped on a street corner of a small town I was passing through, in desperate need of some foot care. I stood for a minute trying to relieve the pain enough to push off again. I walked Charis around the corner and, just like that, I came across a shopfront advertising 'Foot Care'. I stared for a moment, unable to believe my eyes. I hobbled in, thinking there was no way they would be able to see me, but it was worth a try. A dark haired, motherly lady greeted me. "Hi," I said, smiling through the stabbing pain in my foot. "I'm sorry, I don't have an appointment, but the soles of my feet are in a bit of a state and I–." Before I could finish, she was ushering me in. "Come in dear, I've had a couple of cancellations today which is very unusual, so you are in luck."

Marion gave my feet some TLC and whilst she did, we exchanged our stories. She shared her darkest of moments from the life she'd lived. When she spoke, I could feel every word and her story weaved into my bloodstream as though I had waited my whole life to hear it.

Marion had been at home when her husband called her and told her he would be with her soon. He'd just arrived on the ferry from a trip away with Marion's brother on their bikes. It was a regular trip that they took each year, a boys' own adventure. The expected 40-minute travel time passed, and he had not returned. At the time, Marion hadn't considered the importance of the helicopters swirling overhead. It turned out they were lifting her husband to hospital, where he died of his injuries from a road traffic accident caused by a drunk driver. It wasn't just her story, but it was Marion herself that reached into my soul that day. Her journey of healing and moving forwards in a situation that was paved with blame, was humbling. We connected as though we were always meant to meet one another, and it reminded me that what is meant to be will always come to find us. We do not need to have a person in our lives for an eternity to make a deep impact. It is truly down to the power of kindness.

We spent 45 minutes or so together and my feet, while not fixed, were much better. I'm not sure if it was the treatment or the human connection built between us, but I knew now I was recovered enough to carry on.

I took my time along the gravelly canal-side, taking care not to cause more damage to the soles of my feet. The orange hues of the sunset were chasing me down as I moved onto the long, relatively quiet roads ahead. The maths was done, time vs. miles to reach Hull, and the odds weren't in my favour. By the time I reached the iconic Humber Bridge that would take me over to the city, the sun had laid itself down to sleep for the night. As the city's borders emerged so too did the deep darkness. Illuminated by the streetlights, people headed to the warmth of their homes. Aware of how weak my lights were, I pedalled faster to get to the final destination and push through the pain.

The hotel I was booked into was, out of necessity, the cheapest available. It was the oddest hotel I had stayed at yet. I was up and out at the crack of dawn and very happy to be back on the road. It was sunny and bracing as the coolness of the morning hit my face, a great way to wake myself up. I rode through the quiet streets to the cathedral to take my obligatory selfie.

Through social media, I'd been advised by a retired doctor that I should go to York hospital in case I had a hairline fracture in my foot. It would potentially mean a boot would need to be fitted and would most certainly halt the challenge, so it was where I was heading to next.

Before I left Hull, I sought out a place to get an early morning breakfast. I glided Charis through the city centre with ease; barely anyone was awake and the glow of the new dawn was comforting. I love early mornings like this. When you're in a city but no one else is around, you can see the details without distraction. The only place that was open was a fast food place, and I navigated the physical barriers and COVID related registration activities to get inside, finally taking a seat on the squeaky plastic-covered seats. The leftover crumbs on the unclean table did nothing to quell my concerns that I could get COVID from anywhere, despite being extra vigilant and spending the majority of every day alone on the road. I sat waiting for my food to arrive, watching people come and go. Rough sleepers stumbled through the doors, cashing in 'free coffee' cards that they had collected, I imagine, from stickers left on discarded cups. There was a stark contrast to those off to work, grabbing their bacon sarnies in suits. At every stage of my journey, society continued to present all its diversity and inequality. I watched as a small group of homeless men interacted with each other – the paranoia, the sense of unease, all the difficult emotions. I was reminded of the words of an interview I once did: "Solving homelessness is not impossible. But it's not as simple as supplying a home, it's about seeing the whole person and that takes a lot of time."

I crossed paths with another cyclist several times that day. At one point, I found him waiting on a bench in the middle of nowhere on a country backroad. I pulled up. "Hey, I wondered if you might do me a huge favour?" He smiled back, "I will if I can." "Well, I'm doing a world record attempt, and I need witnesses to sign my book. Would you mind?" "No problem." He reached for the book and pen. While he signed the book, he explained why he was sat on a bench in the middle of nowhere. "I'm here waiting for a friend; we meet halfway and ride together from here. This is a good place to stop." As we both looked down across the rolling hills of the landscape, the lush lands of the north, it was clear why. "But he's late; he is always late," he continued, rolling his eyes good naturedly. I took the book from him, loading it back into my bike bag. "Thanks," I said. "I'll be sure if I see your friend along the road, I'll tell him to hurry up! What's their name?" "Sam," he said, with a grin. I jumped back on Charis and glided downhill through the open roads. I had been riding for a while, thinking that Sam was most definitely very late now. Then, a cyclist came bombing along towards me. I shouted out, "You Sam?" He looked confused, and shouted, "Yes?" "Mark says hurry up!" I could see the smile form as he passed at lightning speed.

I arrived in York and headed straight to the hospital. The pain was severe but the knowledge I was somewhere that could help was beyond relieving. As I entered the box-like concrete building, the smiling face of Patrick, a bright and breezy volunteer, greeted me. I found a seat to settle down in, ate snacks and people watched. I knew I didn't know how long I was going to be there, but I was quite happy to sit and stare at the world as it carried on around me. The weight off my feet was like heaven.

After my foot was X-rayed, the doctor confirmed there was no hairline fracture. Amazing. In the clinical hospital setting, I was reminded of a friend and how he found out about his terminal cancer in a most unusual way. He had been on a cycling holiday and had a strong pain in his leg, strong enough for him to go to the doctor about. They ran tests and discovered that he had terminal cancer of the gut.

I didn't share this story with the doctor, so when the doctor asked if there was anything else the matter, my following statement seemed completely out of context. "I have a lump in my breast and I'm not sure if the two issues are related," I said. Underneath the doctor's professional poker face, I could see a hint of confusion. After a pause that was a second too long, he said, "No, no, I think it's fine." He then promptly left to finish the paperwork. I had no time or energy to let the ground swallow me whole, so I just sat on the bed, swinging my legs, looking at the ground while I waited for him to return.

The pain in my feet had started way back on the other side of the country, on an early morning in Manchester. I had been pedalling through the ghost-like city, heading to the cathedral for the obligatory photo. Outside Manchester Cathedral is a stunning statue of a walking Gandhi. The statue gives a powerful message, 'we must take a step forwards to make change'. Just outside of Manchester, I was picking up litter in support of #JustOneBag, a social movement set up in 2020 to collect 2020 bags of rubbish. The target multiplied as the story spread, with thousands of people collecting thousands of bags of rubbish and it now continues year on year with new targets. And it all started with just one bag.

Crossing the peaks to Sheffield was always going to be 40 miles of hell, but the views were something else. The changing colours were so subtle, the new season slowly presenting itself so as not to jar the senses too much when it arrived. Adventurers appeared on hill tops, tiny specks in the distance. However, with all this beauty came pain. The hills were plentiful and so often I felt it was impossible to keep going. I was jumping on and off Charis in an attempt to find ways to cope with the steepness of the landscape. It meant I was pushing off from my foot more often than usual. Up until this point there had been so many obstacles that many of my friends told me they would have already given up. The idea of being forced to give up because of something unrelated to the challenge had not really struck me. That day, as I huffed and puffed up the hills and spent longer than usual to stop and stare across the awe-inspiring views, I allowed my mind to prepare and consider my options if I discovered the lump was something more sinister.

Across those hills, I reached a wonderful place to stop and take five minutes. I decided that really, we all have time to stop and stare, and jump off the bike we're riding, in one way or another. That day, the dappled midday sun cast a softness across the vastness. The colours and contours of the hills rolled into each other as if they were made only for beauty's sake. I jumped back on the ElliptiGO, trudging on to places unexplored and unseen.

By the time I made it to John and Jackie, my next Warm Showers hosts, the sun was setting. I'd reached the outskirts of Sheffield and finished the day with a welcome 5-mile downhill glide. I was exhausted from the journey, not to mention the ongoing pain in my legs, and could barely walk due to my swollen feet. The Merrell shoes I had were the wonderful barefoot style, perfect for the ElliptiGO, but getting on and off so much on the hills had taken its toll. In truth, though, I had been more prepared than ever for all that came. I was distinctly reminded of my cycle across America, when I had not been prepared at all.

# Chapter 10

## Cycling across America: 2018

## "Winning a sofa on your birthday."

On day 24 of my cycle across the States, I set off with high hopes from a Loves truck stop in Texas. Every time I walked into a Loves petrol station, the same voice rang over the Tannoy, chiming: *"Welcome to Loves!"* It was a familiar inflection which stuck in my mind, not annoying per se, but more like a favourite song ear-worming its way into your head. I knew the road would be long, flat and very, very, very straight. On the map it looked brilliant, an absolute joy. I expected it be the easiest day imaginable.

Thinking back to the long, Texan roads I'd so often seen in the movies, I always thought how much I'd love to drive them, lost in thought, with cool tunes playing on the radio. Now I could live that dream. Ahead of me was a single road with vast wastelands either side. There were occasional abandoned buildings in the middle of the land, no crops growing, and no signs of life. The air was muggy, the sun held back by a thin sheen of cloud. I stopped to eat, and the silence was deafening. There was nothing and I felt so far away from even myself. Places that had names on the map turned out to be just a small set of abandoned buildings, nowhere at all really. It was if the world stopped and all the people had just upped and left.

During the first three hours of cycling, I kept watching the horizon, thinking, *I'll be there in a moment, I'll be at that horizon.* However, it never seemed to arrive. I was chasing something down that was impossible to reach. My very own pot of gold at the end of rainbow. In all that time, only three vehicles had passed me on the road. One vehicle for each long hour. The constant chase for the impossible had drained me. The hope I had been carrying from the morning had seeped out onto the long straight roads and curled up in the thick warm afternoon air. I dreaded to think what would have happened if I hadn't started the day with a surge of positivity. My phone signal dropped out at around the same time as the road surface disintegrated into rough gravel. After a further five miles I got a single bar of signal and called James, who picked me up. Tears that had threatened but hadn't come, streaked down my cheeks unashamedly. I sobbed and sobbed until there was nothing left. I'd had enough. I felt a failure for not being able to make the last 15 miles. Was what I was doing worth it? Was I just a stupid person who was out of her depth? Would the challenge actually make a difference to the world?

We all have a place in our minds that unlocks when we are beyond exhaustion; a numbness that would almost be pleasurable if it wasn't for the trauma that causes it. I have to say there is a euphoria that comes. It is mixture of your body shutting down, not only physically but mentally, to protect you. What I learnt that day is if you let it and trust it, you will recover. I think if I fought it, I might have kept fighting and failed. Of course, there was undoubtedly a self-made pressure to achieve my self-set goal. However, having goals provide us with purpose, they stretch our abilities, build our resilience and allow us to learn more about ourselves.

I had never done any research on how to achieve goals. I never found an easy to follow, tried and tested route in life or even in my career in leadership. Accomplishing the goals I set myself was a gradual process and I learnt through my own mistakes. The idea of achieving our goals starts with believing in ourselves, but it's the practicalities which push the dream into reality. What do I need? What are all the actions I need to take to make this possible? Do I need money? Do I need support? What do I need to learn? What is the point? When those questions get answered, you can start to plan a route towards the goal. I try to not think too much about the end, instead simply focusing on each action that drives me forward. There are of course changes which happen and are out of our control, but we can usually find a way around them if we want it bad enough.

As I moved into day 25, I had to make up the miles I had missed the day before, so I headed back from the town we were in, to the point where I had given up. I was quiet, considered, but equally shattered, pondering my choices. The previous afternoon of rest had given me some much-needed mental space. I stopped listening to what others were saying and tuned into me and my thoughts. I decided I would no longer measure my miles with the speedometer. The idea of watching the numbers tick by felt like the worst thing to do, despite it being recommended.

Setting off on the morning of day 26 I knew I needed to get ahead. I was quite a few days behind and to get back on track I needed to reshape my mindset. The pressure to succeed was still ever present, but I had stopped listening to others and tuned into my own thoughts, who I was, and what I needed to motivate my heart. So, while getting prepped I made a subtle change to the usual routine. I carefully set the speedometer to track mileage but placed it in the panniers so I couldn't see it. I pushed on through the long, ever-so-slightly winding roads, which flowed with gradual assents and descents that cars never notice but for cyclists feel momentous. More life began to present itself out in the scattered towns. The roads were quiet in the main and I was able to listen to music to lift my spirits and ease the ache of failure that I carried.

After some time, I stopped and refuelled myself not because I was hungry (or bored, a common side effect of so many miles) but simply because I wanted something nice to eat. I delved into my panniers and as I bought out some food, I also checked how far I'd come. I guessed 20 miles. I was wrong. According to the speedometer, I'd covered more than twice the miles I thought I had. I had to keep looking, to check it was right. My heavy heart was starting to lift.

That day I hadn't aimed to get to anywhere in particular, I was just going to ride until I'd had enough or there was a good place to stop. This just so happened to be at 80 miles. I'd cycled them without even thinking about it. I saw the support van pulled over in a picnic area in the middle of nowhere and I stopped for the day. James was editing footage in the back of the van. As I sat in the front snacking, he suggested I might want to go on a little longer as it was still a few hours until sunset. "Ah no, I won't," I said. "Well, the wind is in your favour and you could do your first century ride," he said.

I mulled it over. I knew I could do it, but did I want to? It would take me an hour and half to make up those 20 miles, and the sun was due to set in two. It was now or never. I went for it. The roads were rolling, and I pushed every last ounce of my energy through those pedals. I made the decision and that was it.

As I whizzed along the road with a new confidence that I had gained that day, the wind at my back, I saw a man standing outside of a van, clearly waiting for me to pass. I felt a little uneasy as I approached, but saw he was holding up bottles of water to give to me.

"Hi," he said as I slowed. "I saw you up the road. I've done some support before for people doing the Southern Route. I know how important the water is in these areas where there are no people or shops."

"Wow, thank you so much, that's so kind," I said, taking some water. "Yeah, we have a 60-mile round trip to the nearest big supermarket now, so when we shop, we have to shop for at least a month." I imagined the van packed to the rafters with groceries. "We like to support the cyclists," he said. "What are you doing, anyway?" I explained my mission to encourage the international conversation on kindness. After I told him I was shooting for 100 miles, he told me there was a picnic stop just 10 miles ahead that would round off my first century ride. "That's great, thank you so much," I said, "I'll head off! I might get there before dark if I'm quick!"

As the gloom was descending upon the day, I pushed through, the wind on my back. I went as fast as I could – my drive to reach the end was greater than ever. As I rounded the chicane, the picnic area, a bench with cover, presented itself. While the sun was gone, there was enough of the evening glow to see there was a bottle of water on the table with a note of encouragement from the man I had met just 10 miles previous, a touching act to finish my first 100-mile day.

The next day, the weather turned. A storm descended, and the wind changed direction. The air was heavy with anticipation; you could feel it before you even heard the cracks of lightning that lit up the land. The open, flat lands gave no cover for the bolts that struck from floor to ceiling on the world's canvas. In time, I came over and through rocky cliff faces. On the other side of the canyon the land opened back up again. The layered hills in the distance produced every shade of brown you could imagine, a phenomenon of light and shadow. I continued towards the horizon.

Up ahead, I could see a big truck creeping along with a couple of guys shovelling stuff off of the road and into the back. At first, it looked like roadworks. As I got closer, I soon realised that what they were shovelling was roadkill – to be precise, hares, huge hares. Some of them, with their ears included, would have been as high as my hip. As I passed the truck, I saw the road ahead was covered in dead hares, while hundreds more hopped around in the desert wasteland. How many, I wondered, had died at the hands of the truck drivers travelling this way? There was a lot of time to think on the bike and the cruelness did not pass me by.

"How are you getting on?" I heard James' voice at the other end of the phone. "Oh, ok, what's up?" I asked as I continued to pedal. "I'm waiting by the side of the road, very near the border. I found a place to film; I think you'll love it."

Now the sun was constant, driving heat and sunburn into my skin. We were about to arrive in Del Rio for the night. I spotted James' van on the endless straight road sometime before I made it to him. I pulled in, following him by foot through shrubland, navigating the rocky surface with care. Then the landscape opened up into a long deep valley. The sound though, was so loud I was barely able to think. It sounded as if every bird in the world was calling to each other, desperately trying to be heard over the cawing, tweeting and screeching. You didn't just hear it; it rose up and wound its way into the core of your very being. You became one with it. The bottom of the valley was filled with trees and undergrowth, the happiest city for all wildlife. They appeared unafraid and uninfluenced by humans. You could stand on one side of the valley and look across at the other side, teetering above the vast array of life swarming deep in the valley but unable to see it through the thick undergrowth.

One side was America and the other was Mexico. It was a memorable and sobering location.

I didn't want to leave; I wanted to sit and listen to the birdsong echo through the valley. An inner peace washed over me. The almost Jurassic sounds seemed so alien to our busy, urban world and it was music to my ears. I wanted to lay on the rock and soak up the sun, forgetting everything else. Living in the present is easy when we're in a place that we love to be. For most of my life and indeed the challenge, I had felt a constant need to rush, as if time was running out. This was the first place on the journey where time stood still, just for a moment, before I had to keep going and stick to the promise I'd made; not just to the people supporting me, but to myself.

Before heading off from England I had contacted a tonne of media and press outlets, but it was surprisingly difficult to get any attention if you're not raising cold hard cash. Things aren't meant to be easy; people want to see figures. The point of my work is to change this. Anyway, the Del Rio New Herald had been more interested than most. By email, they said they would meet me, interview me and write up a story. They even told me that the Chamber of Commerce had an event I was invited to at the Falcon Art Gallery, which would be held the following day – incidentally, on my birthday.

Day 30, despite being my birthday, didn't quite go to plan. The van broke down, but I decided while it was at the mechanics being fixed, I'd take advantage of the good weather and cycle as far as I could before having to head back to Del Rio. It meant I could give myself a head start on the mileage for tomorrow.

With my time up, I turned around to head back, taking note of the location I had reached. I had planned enough time to pick up the van and make my evening commitments.

The clock ticked inside of me, a growing sense of unrest that comes from needing to be somewhere at a certain time. I knew that it was going to be tight to get back to town in time. The long straight roads and sun's rays made for a pleasant day, however as I turned and stood on the other side of the road, I hoped someone might pick me up and lo and behold, they did. A big white pick-up pulled up just in front of me and a very Texan couple jumped out to see if I was ok and ask if I might want a lift. I jumped in and the bike went into the back. As we travelled down the road, a sense of ease fell over me... Something mixed with safety and relief that I would meet the time restraints that chained me. We got chatting. They were off to get their boat out of storage and would pass just a few miles outside of Del Rio. They owned a farm, but the wife was also a teacher. She said the story of the challenge I was doing would be great for her children. The hum of stories continued throughout the journey. When we pulled up just a few miles out of Del Rio I realised how attached I had become to them. Good people continued to present themselves.

The Falcon Art Gallery sits on a crossroads on the outskirts of the city. A low bungalow style building, it is wooden with a garden and porch that runs around the perimeter, sort of a converted house, if you like. I approached through the gate as people milled in the garden and approached the long registration table.

"If y'all just leave your business card in the bowl, y'all be entered into our raffle," said the lady at the table. As it happened, the cards got picked from a hat to win prizes, from a $500 voucher for a sofa company to a bottle of BBQ sauce.

I continued into the garden as people milled around chatting, networking, interacting. There was a BBQ and a long table of food. I met up with the New Herald journalist who proceeded to introduce me to a flurry of people. They asked me, as always, about my trip and work, and I listened to them give their opinions and thoughts on kindness. When you mention kindness, stories of kindness and people's opinions on it always follow. It is why I call myself an accidental researcher of kindness. I just couldn't stop people sharing, but why would I ever want to?

The evening showcased the art of children from less fortunate countries whom the owner of the gallery had worked with. Their work was telling, sharing a story of a different world. The gallery owner seemed a truly selfless man. We all aspire in some way to be like that, but many of us never achieve it. He had.

To my delight I won a raffle prize, but a sofa at this point in my life was sadly no good to me so it went back into the hat. I barely had room for an extra pair of shoes let alone furniture.

My birthday has an undercurrent of unease about it, not because of another year passed by but simply because of a memory that will never fade from that time. It was the beginning of March 2012, a month before my birthday. I walked in the front door from a day at work. The smell of cooking wafted towards me and the TV hummed in the background. I walked through the living room into the kitchen to find Paul making dinner. With some joke or quick wit, he came over to pull me into his warm embrace. After some time and too soon for me, he pulled back, held my face, looked at my eyes and kissed me. I can feel the day as if it was only yesterday. He turned and moved back to what he was doing while we chatted about our respective days. Paul then asked the killer question that most people find tough to answer, "What do you want for your birthday?"

It was really an impossible question. We had planned to have his son to stay for a few weeks over my birthday at the end of March and I was excited for the road trip to pick him up from Europe where he lived. I told Paul, "Our plans are enough, I really don't want anything." The conversation continued over the following week as I continued to insist, I was really happy. with nothing; I was just happy to have a week off with him.

Paul died three weeks later on the 23rd March 2012. My birthday was exactly one week later, and we never reached our long-awaited time off. A friend who had come to the house in the first few days told me that before his death, Paul had contacted her. He had bought us a Spa Day at a place she recommended. He had written in the final email to her that he wouldn't tell me until the very last minutes of my birthday so I could believe that I got 'bugger all as she had asked for'. I think when he died, it changed my DNA. Something in the core of me, the carefreeness that I carried, seemed to seep from me like water from a sieve. The person I was with him never existed again.

The next 10 days went by in a fog of Texan miles. Texas is a pretty diverse state but there are large areas of nothing and then the occasional tiny, abandoned place where no one lives, the classic 'ghost town'. I wondered about the stories of those who had lived there. Where they had gone? What had happened? Had they just died off?

The roads were quiet, and I wondered if the arrival of the highways meant that as less people passed through these towns' things had just shut up. As I rode my bike and saw the world from a quiet observer's viewpoint, I started to wonder if we are really able to see the long-term legacy of what we leave behind.

I passed farm upon farm as I rode the last 800 miles out of Texas. The land awe inspiring and dull in equal measure. Every few miles or so I would pass large, gated farm entrances, a world existing beyond them far from the one I occupied today. I had been going for days, attempting to catch up on myself. I was about halfway through the entire ride and had pushed on regardless. However, it could not continue. I had started to stop every mile or so and was now walking up the mildest of hills. My body felt heavy and my mind foggy. I thought I was simply bored, but it was in fact my body telling me it was time to stop.

As I stood by the side of the road the only sounds were the crickets and the distant sound of an approaching vehicle. The car passed and pulled up ahead. A man got out the driver's seat and started to walk towards me,

"Everything ok ma'am?"    "Oh yes, thank you. Just struggling today."    I went onto explain what I was aiming to do. "I don't think I have far to go now." I said with some optimism. "I cycle too," he said. "Maybe you have simply 'hit the wall'."

With that, the penny dropped.

# Chapter 11

## ElliptiGO World Record Challenge: 2020

### "Never give up, even when it appears pointless to continue!"

A few years later, in a different country on a different mode of transport, I was travelling over a section of the Yorkshire Dales that was, for the most part, 46 uphill miles. I knew it would be a new level of hell. Although the scenery was out of this world, I just hoped I could reach the end as I huffed, puffed, and on occasion walked up hills that had a gradient I couldn't even understand.

Finding somewhere to stay had been tough too. It was only the day before reaching the Dales that I came across a place called the 'Old School Bunk House' near Hawes. It housed 26 people with everything you could need: six bedrooms full of bunks, a huge kitchen, and a living room. It was a long shot, but I contacted them. I was welcome to stay there for the night, free of charge. There would be nobody else there, because of the Pandemic. With so few options it was an incredible gift, and even more so because I would have so much space.

As I pushed up on up the hill, the sat nav saying I was just metres away, I passed a man and a young child playing in a garden. I smiled to myself. The Old School Bunk House was actually right next door to their house. It was a long, old stone building with a large sign letting me know I'd arrived. As I continued up the hill and into the car park, I imagined what it would have been like when it was the local school. Today though, it was a roof over my head, and I could breathe a sigh of relief.

I opened the lockbox using the code I'd been given, retrieving the key. I turned the key in the lock and as it clicked open my breath expelled all of the unease I had felt on the uphill cycle. I peered down the long corridor with all of the rooms coming off and set Charis just inside the entrance, so I was ready to go in the morning. I poked my head into the rooms and as my mind took me through all the things I needed to do next. I felt that there was something missing. I had previously not required a sleeping bag and the quick-dry towel I'd had back on the road I had left at a previous host's because I didn't need it. However, I needed it now. These bunkhouses don't generally provide bedding or towels and so suddenly I started to think through what I might do. I knew I could sleep in my clothes for warmth and use something I had as a towel. None of it was impossible but as I was travelling with so little, it would be chilly, that was for sure.

After a little thought, I walked back to the house next door to see if the family might have anything they could lend me. Not ideal by any stretch of the imagination. COVID was still very much present and while I had barely any contact with anyone and when I did it was following the rules, I did not in any way want to upset anyone by asking for unsolicited help. I approached with care and the man who I had seen outside just minutes ago was now sorting something in his van.

"Hi, I am so sorry to disturb you," I said. "This is a little bit of an odd request. However, I am doing this World Record on a stand-up bike, 5000 miles through every city. I just went past you." He didn't confirm or deny, he just stared at me. "Anyway," I carried on, "I couldn't find a place to stay up here in the sticks, but the owners of the bunk house have kindly put a roof over my head tonight. But I'm in a pickle, as I'm not carrying a sleeping bag or a towel, I wondered if there was anything you might have that you'd be happy to lend me? Anything would do."

Stoically and without emotion he said, "Let me see if we have something." And with that he turned and went.

While he was gone, I felt terrible for asking. I kept wishing I had everything I needed and didn't have to ask for help. When the man returned with a towel and sleeping bag my heart warmed in my chest and I beamed a smile. "Thank you so much, that is incredible." I passed him a card with the details of Sunshine People on it. "This is what I'm doing, just so you know, and I'll be sure to drop back your things in the morning. Thank you so much again, I am so grateful."

I took the short walk back to the bunkhouse, got a shower, made up some food and got myself settled. It felt scary to be in the house on my own. It was just so much space to fill and I suddenly felt so very small.

The knock-knock on the door made me jump. My heart was pounding. There was no one planning to come and meet me, and the owners would not come for 48 hours because of COVID rules. I was on edge. I tiptoed down the long corridor. "Who's there?" I shouted through the solid wooden door. "Oh, hello, I'm the man from next door."

"Oh hi, I am so sorry, one moment…" I garbled as I opened up the door. "My wife found your social media page and wondered if any of this might help."

I stared at the man in grateful disbelief. His arms were laden with supplies. His wife had sent a number of goodies for me, food and beverages as well as painkillers and ibuprofen gel. They had seen from the updates that I had foot pain. Yet again, the power of love and people's ability to connect astounded me. We all have the extraordinary power to be kind, and if we used it daily, what would the world look like I wonder? I settled down for the night, a little less scared and lot more cared for.

I set off the next day, returning my borrowed items to the neighbours and leaving a heartfelt thank you note. I headed for the town of Hawes, the well-known top spot of the Dales. At the top of the next hill, there was a layby where a gentleman was changing his boots to head off for a walk. I passed slowly because of the gradient and he made a comment about the ElliptiGO. I always try to stop to speak to as many people as possible, so I pulled in. The man had kipped in the car after dropping his daughter at University and wanted to stop for a walk on the way through. When I left, I felt more engaged, and felt sure that the day's ride would not be as bad as I had imagined.

You know what? That was exactly how it was. The sun shone and what should have a been a tough day with many hills was glorious. I felt as if I was flying. I rolled with the hills and delighted in the smooth road surface, the low light and shadows comforting and inspiring me. I felt the vastness of the land surrounding me, with each turn bringing something new and wonderful. I didn't want it to end. Well, ok, maybe I wanted the cycling to end, but the views, the perfect light… I want it to go on forever.

Finding and arranging places to stay was generally a challenge. Darlington had been no exception. I'd looked on Warm Showers and wrote to a number of hosts, but the timing was off, including a guy who was away in Scotland at the time. When he apologised, I had said it was absolutely fine and I would figure something out and wished them well on their vacation. While I wondered what to do, thinking out a solution, he wrote back and told me he had booked me into a local hotel and that he hoped I enjoyed it. A person I had never met, who knew little about my work or life or what I was trying to achieve, had decided to make my life a little easier.

51 days into the challenge and this was the first day that nothing had gone wrong; a good summary of the challenge overall. I arrived at the beautiful hotel and followed my usual routine; getting Charis to a safe place, working out if I could do any washing (or better still, drying), making food, showering, rubbing magnesium lotion into my legs, stretching. That night I watched TV to numb myself from the overwhelming feeling of not being worthy of the kindness shown to me. Was I just some pointless middle-aged woman on a bike? My feet and legs were in pain, the lump in my breast was now showing through my clothes. Was the world telling me I shouldn't be doing this? Would it all be worth it?

As I rode towards Darlington, the sun shining, I started to think about the ever-changing environment. The Pandemic meant I had to consider pausing the challenge and starting again when things were more certain. I needed to ensure I kept people safe and followed the law, so I mapped out all my options. The news was wild with what would and could happen next as I started to consider where I could leave Charis and get home to wait out another lockdown.

And, amongst all of these thoughts, I was suddenly aware of the number of thank you cards I wanted to send. So, as I arrived into Newcastle, I popped into the post office in High Felling.

I handed over my thank you cards that I had been writing along the way. "I'd like to send these please." There was a silent nod of agreement from the lady behind the counter, and then she asked, "So, what are you doing? We saw you ride up on the cameras." As she delved into her large stamp book, I went on to explain the challenge, where I'd been and where I was going. "The thank you cards are for some of the people that have helped me along the way." There was some chatter between the two ladies behind each window who admired the challenge. Off I went, bidding them farewell.

As I was walking out through the sweets section, I wondered if I should treat myself. I knew I needed to be careful about the amount of sugar I put into my body, but as I so often told myself, *I shouldn't, but I'm going to.*

Anyway, I was near the front door, perusing the sweets, and the shop owner approached me. "Do you need to use the bathroom at all, is there anything we can help with?" For once I didn't and besides, I would be at the hotel very soon. "Ah, that's kind, I'm actually ok."

The shop owner asked me what I was looking for. "Oh," I said, "I shouldn't really have sugar, but I fancy a treat." "Oh, we have sugar-free sweets!" A bag was promptly given to me for my journey. It was a tiny act, but I left feeling that even if everything fell apart around me, the people of the UK would inspire me to complete the challenge. It wasn't just a bag of sweets; it was another example of finding connection through kindness.

As I left the Post Office, I rolled down a sloping hill. I could see Newcastle in the distance. I knew where I was heading and prayed that I wouldn't have to cycle up hills like this tomorrow. I wanted to enjoy the downward hills so much, but I knew too much now about the contours of the land as I neared the halfway mark. For every easy slope down was an excruciating climb up.

Arriving at the Hilton Hotel, I entered the almost stately drop off area; a square shape surrounded by three sides of the imposing building. In this enclosed area, flags flew and a mini roundabout with a fountain gave a message of grandeur. Rolling up on Charis, I was already out of place.

As we entered the large foyer, I could see a floor-to-ceiling glass wall with a clear view of the iconic Gateshead bridge, with a veranda for guests to enjoy drinks. An indoor water feature and the modern chandelier light created a sense of luxury. At the reception desk, I was greeted by the manager and team. While I was visually out of place, the team was comforting and gave me a sense of belonging which was often so far away when I was floundering on my own out on the roads. As Charis was safely stored away, I was escorted to my room.

When the Hilton colleague opened my door for me, I gasped audibly. The room that I was presented with was a spacious apartment. Beyond the floor to ceiling glass windows, I could see the Gateshead Bridge. I walked a little further into the room. A table in the centre of the living space had been laden with all the snacks and drinks I could possibly want. After the colleague left, I wandered into a bathroom I could fit a couple of football teams in and probably play a game in too. I caught a glimpse of myself in the huge mirror and realised my mouth was still hanging open in shock.

That evening, I was signed up to deliver a talk. Achieving the 5000 miles, encouraging acts of kindness, and meeting the work commitments that kept my business afloat was a juggling act. It felt like I was holding onto everything by my fingertips.

The following day I left late. I only had 23 miles to go, so made the most of the suite and views. I hoped that the rain might take a break, but it was relentless by the time I set off in the afternoon. The dark clouds and freezing cold torrential rain made it look and feel like night.

I was drenched by the time I got to the next hotel on the outskirts of a place called Acomb. I felt completely done in. They had no drying facilities, so I had to prioritise what went on the radiator. A mild contentment washed over me.

Exhausted, cold, drenched and lacking in so many things we take for granted, my body slumped onto the bed. I dragged myself up to make a cup of tea and ripped open the complimentary biscuits. I took a deep breath, and with each exhale a little more of the exhaustion left me. I sunk down into the covers to get warm and conked out.

The Pandemic restrictions were chasing me down. Scotland had taken a lead with new COVID legislation, and I was praying I could get into the country before they shut down travel. Every day I adapted my plans to meet the changing rules, working out what to do if I needed to pause the challenge and restart later down the line, whenever that would be.

I set off the next morning in freezing fog. The hills were their usual unforgiving selves, giving nothing and taking everything in those difficult early miles. The roads opened up and I was then riding the long straight roads with parts of Hadrian's Wall appearing intermittently.

The roads stretched as far as the eye could see, flowing like waves as the long straight road followed the contours of the landscape.

I followed the Hadrian's Wall path and gained an official wall path stamp, something walkers collect as evidence of trudging the entire wall. I continued. The rolling hills that followed Hadrian's Wall were now much more daunting. Then the rain came, just 10 miles from the end, and it arrived in all its glory. It had wanted to rain all day, but I think it had been storing it up and decided to let it all out over the next hour. The droplets were so thick I was barely able to see in front of me, puddles soon merging to flood the road as I pushed on.

My final destination was to Denise and John's. I had also stayed with them on my 500-mile walk in 2019. Denise had been the one who told me about the book festival I'd then gone on to speak at later that year. I had liked Denise and John very much the first time around and knew that nothing would change. They were welcoming and easy going. There was a wonderful dynamic between them that allowed their individual personalities to shine through. Approaching the house, I walked down the long and gravelly path. It was too dangerous to ride — the stones and potholes were precarious in normal weather, but in the rain they were impossible. I reached the house, waddled into the porch and rung the bell. I was soaked through despite all the waterproofs and I wondered how I was going to even enter the house. The door opened and after some delight at the bike and my endeavour, Denise and John whipped into practical support mode.

I felt the safety of the familiar easiness and kindness once again. "I've got some ferrets now." John told me with a grin. So, as we walked down to the barn with the ElliptiGO, out came the ferrets to say hello. We stood in the barn for a while, talking about the mechanics of the bike as John oiled the chain for me. The evening was spent with the warmth of the Aga seeping into my bones. The food warmed my heart and the conversation energised my soul; a conversation about family and life and work. Easy and enjoyable, the best kind of conversation.

The next morning the rain stayed away but the cold came to replace it. I felt like we had missed autumn and gone straight into winter. I set off up the gravel road, walking first to the main road. John followed in his truck to see me off and also satisfy his curiosity about the bike. While I couldn't see it as I rode off, I could feel his smile and the shake of his head in disbelief as the reality of what I was doing sunk in for him.

I was due to travel 67 miles. It was a huge day under any circumstances as I was heading into Scotland then cycling west to pick up the ferry in the port at Cairnryan. This milestone was some 120 miles away and I had found a Warm Showers to put me up about halfway. It looked like it might be the last home from home I'd be able to stay at for a while. The talk in the Scottish media suggested this option would, within days, no longer be available, as people would no longer be able to stay in someone else's property even with suitable measures in place. Not having anywhere to stay could easily derail the challenge, but I was trying to stick within the law and also ensure people were safe. All I could do was wait for the news and make the necessary changes as I went. It felt huge but not impossible, I just had to step up my game.

The houses became more plentiful as I travelled on the road, a familiar path from my walk the year before. Back then, this stretch of road was my final day. Today I was only half-way on my journey. The sign for Carlisle presented itself and I was officially heading from England into Scotland. I was due to be greeted by Davina, an old friend from many years ago. When I saw Davina enthusiastically waving outside of the cathedral with her bubbly, easy going smile, I broke down and cried. It was all too much; the mounting pressure, the relief of a familiar face, the encouragement and thoughtfulness of my friend, the endless day that lay ahead. It felt so good to free some of the tears that had been building inside of me.

We wandered around the cathedral and took the required photo and just like that I was off again. I would have liked to have stayed longer, sat on the wall and chatted about life, but time would not allow.

Arriving in Gretna Green always feels a little odd. It's a place of something and nothing. Everyone knows it, it has history and a story but no character. It's busy but feels like it has no soul. However, I was due to complete an ITV interview there. I was pushing hard to get there on time. I kept watching the clock as I tackled the wind. The roads, for the most part, were relatively quiet. As I passed the vast landscape and the old train lines, my mind kept circling back to the worry of being late and when I arrived, I realised I had not thought about what I was going to say. By the time I got there my mind was blank. It turned out to be the worst interview I have ever done.

I headed west. The weather had taken a turn for the worse and it was freezing. It was only early September but in Scotland my cycling gloves were not even close to keeping out the cold that was increasing.

Eventually, I popped into a Tesco in Annan. As usual I took Charis with me, parking her at security and explaining what I was doing and why. I got chatting to Joe, a Tesco employee. After a wander round, I wandered out having used the toilet and bought a packet of 'on offer' biscuits to have as a treat later.  Joe asked, "Is there anything we can get you? The manager says we'd like to support you." "That's so nice, thank you, but I think I'm set actually."  There was a feeling of warmth that washed over me as I rode away, and with that the cold wind whipped through me and bit at my fingers.  I wondered if maybe they could help with that. I thought about it, and my mind said, "No, I'll be ok."

As I continued on and the headwind reared up in my face, I turned around and headed back to them. There was an awkward moment of finding Joe again, to ask him if in fact the manager might have some gloves they could give to me. They did, and I left with a pair of thick warm gloves. It was a little slice heaven, the warmth from my heart now extended into my hands. Such a small thing, but it renewed my inner strength.

I pushed on but felt like I wasn't getting very far against the headwind. I made it to Dumfries and popped into a café. It was late lunch and my energy levels were waning, I needed fuel. Once I sat down, I realised I had nothing left in the tank, even after having some food. I was done. I was 25 miles short and exhausted, so I made the tough decision to book a B&B. A wonderful Sunshine Person had donated money for a room and the timing could not have been more perfect.

I headed straight to the B&B and was welcomed with a smile and a free breakfast for the following morning. The owner had seen my story aired on the news. She came to knock on the door to tell me how wonderful she thought it was. I smiled graciously but in truth even that was a struggle.

The following day I would have to get to the port for check-in by 2.30pm for a 3.30pm crossing, or wait for the later ferry at 8pm, meaning a very late arrival into Belfast. I needed to catch that 3.30pm ferry, but 75 miles was a struggle even on a good day. I was averaging 10 mph and so whichever way I looked at it, the maths just didn't stack up. But I think we have established by now that I was always willing to give it a go, so I rested and prepared myself for what was to come. While the bed and room were glorious, I slept fitfully knowing the next day would be a difficult one. With decreasing energy, I felt a new level of weakness, but there was only one way to go: forwards.

I woke early and should have got straight on the road. The time was going to be tight and the early start would have helped, but I stayed for breakfast because food is fuel and when someone kindly offers you a free meal you should always do your best to accept.

I managed to get on the road for 8am. It was sunny with a biting chill in the air that burned the skin on my face. I put on my nice, new, warm gloves and my waterproofs to help take the edge off.

I was on a mission, although I felt anything but strong enough to manage it. I set off uphill upon hill, I felt weak and already wanted to give up. So, I decided to start talking to myself for encouragement. "I am strong, I am strong, I am strong." Before I knew it, I was 10 miles in and past the worst of the elevation. It was working!

People I met along the way often said, "You must be enjoying the scenery!" In truth, most days I missed it. The hills, bad road surface, rain or headwinds were usually enough to distract me from the passing landscape. Today, though, I didn't feel the need to think about all the things I had to do or the people I had to call. I didn't think about filming and I didn't feel guilt for not doing any. I just rode like a demon with my mantra: I am strong. It was an extraordinary day, one that pushed the limits of my abilities and clarified the power of my internal chatter and the stories I tell myself. What we say to each other matters, but what we say to ourselves impacts everything we do.

I kept going until I got to a garage. I only had six miles to go but it was too late. I had little chance finishing the last six miles in 15 minutes. I admitted defeat, but in so many ways I had won.

My cycle was now less urgent, but I still wanted to get there and for the day's riding to be done. After stocking up on snacks at the garage and taking time to rest, I continued on. Coming down the hill towards the port, I could see a ferry just pulling away. A feeling of confusion swept over me; my brain was unable to compute. The ferry should have long gone. It dawned on me that there may have been a delay. I knew there was nothing I could do now, but a sense of missing the boat sunk deep into my psyche. I continued down the hill onto the long straight road running along the sea into the port. The afternoon sun bounced off the water to my left and the windows of the houses to my right. I pulled up to the terminal and went inside. There was no one around and nothing in the room except a vending machine. A person stepped out of a door and crossed the foyer where I sat. "Hi, can I ask, was the last ferry delayed?" "Yeah, it was quite delayed, just left a little while ago." And they entered into another door as I said, "Ok, thanks."

This was an important lesson for me to learn the hard way: never give up, even when you think it's pointless. You just never know. This was something I should have understood well enough from cycling across America. Now I know every lesson often comes in different forms, albeit with the same outcome.

# Chapter 12

## Cycling across America: 2018

### "The sunshine state!"

I left the couple by the side of the road with the term 'hit the wall' swimming in my mind. Not much further on, I met up with James at a deserted petrol station on a crossroads with nothing else for miles around. I was both mentally and physically drained and unable to get any further. I climbed into the back of the van to sleep. I woke an hour later to a tapping on the side of the van. I slid open the door, rubbing the sleep out of my eyes.

Strangely, there were a couple of peacocks strutting around at this petrol station in the middle of nowhere. They walked with confidence and seemed to know not to stray into the road, staying close to the surrounding building and small picnic area. When they got up close to the van and saw their reflection, they would try to peck at it and therefore the van. I shooed them away and took a closer look at where I was.

There was a rickety outbuilding made of wooden frame, with netting to act as walls. Just behind this, up a slightly less rickety wooden ramp, was a toilet and a sink. I made an assessment and through my tiredness went about doing the daily tasks that needed to be done: handwashing clothes in the sink, cooking some food, strip washing in the bathroom that had seen better days and, on occasion, trying to chase the peacocks away from the van.

Everything was too much, each tiny chore too big a task, but they all had to be done. Night fell quickly without any notice at all. With it came moths, thousands upon thousands of them, each as big as my thumb. They swarmed and covered the night sky. I pondered where they had all come from. It was fascinating to watch them frenzy around the lights of our small camp. As I went to the loo before bed, the idea of them getting caught in my hair gave me a strange sense of fear – given the choice it was something I'd rather avoid. I wasn't aware of just how much the constant waves of fear (albeit small) were impacting me and wouldn't for another week or so.

Every state in America has a uniqueness to it, each a country in itself and screaming to tell its own unique story. By about day 40 I was finally out of Texas and felt like I was really moving now. I was crossing states in a few days. Texas had nearly killed me. As I came out into Louisiana, I sighed with relief.

In New Orleans, I was only 12 days from the end of the challenge, but I had been going for 45 days and the build-up of everything, both mentally and physically, had taken its toll. I had an emotional breakdown. It was only fortunate I was on a day off when it happened. Talking was hard, as was breathing. My brain shut down. The long-term effects of being in a state of fight or flight for so long were showing through my attempts to stay sane.

Now, perhaps there is something to be said for a complete breakdown, because the next day I would cycle my furthest daily distance. It seems that the ride really was turning out to be rollercoaster. I was now firmly out of the long straight roads, hitting towns often. I was becoming more aware of my surroundings. As I hit the last 20 miles of the day, the cycle paths that had started to appear were welcome. However, as day turned to night, I became conscious of the bog land where the crocodiles lived. I had never pedalled so hard. When I made it to the town where we would stay, I realised I'd completed an unexpected 120 miles. It turns out that James' longest day of cycling had been 119 miles and he seemed quite happy to admit this, maybe to make up for the sometimes-sceptical outlook he had previously portrayed and to give me a boost after my recent meltdown. Either way, I was happy to just eat and get to sleep as quickly as possible. I was now quite unwell. The pain had been gradual, but on some days, debilitating. It mostly hit in the morning or at night, when I stopped, and my body had time to catch up.

As I hit the Florida coast, the sun was shining down on me. People were enjoying their vacations at the bustling restaurants I passed. The roads were busy with a slowness that holiday makers bring. The atmosphere was calm and I for one was soaking it all up. I stopped at a public toilet in a car park and discovered blood. I wasn't sure if it was a gut issue or the ongoing stress. For the entire trip, when I needed to go to the toilet, I had to go. The roads had taken their toll on my gut. After six weeks, it had had enough.

I continued to follow the coast as much as possible. The towns and beaches started to get more touristy but with a touch of class. The beaches, with their white sands rolling into far distances and flat landscapes, were paradise.

I was just five days from the end. The weather turned, bringing a sudden torrential rainstorm. I took the day to rest, stuck between reading and sleeping, lying in the back of the van and listening to the rain pelt onto the roof. My body needed to feel some safety, and to rest.

After my rest day, I managed another 101-mile cycle, again more by accident than by design. The roads were flat, and I was rolling in and out of the coastline. I had gotten into a rhythm and before I knew it, I was over 100 miles in and had not seen James yet. I called him, and he admitted he was still over two hours away. I managed to find a trailer park that offered me use of the shower, but with no towel or wash stuff I declined. The sun was going down when James turned up several hours later. I was cold from the sudden chill after a day of cycling in the sun.

When I think of those last few days, I should have been more excited to see the end, but it didn't seem to be getting any easier. It was a hard push to get those final miles under my belt.

I rode along the Mississippi Gulf Coast for the following five days and it was glorious. The sun shone, the winds stilled, and the roads were smoother as Florida arrived. As I approached the Pensacola Peninsula, I met James at a car park, and we decided it was time to eat. I wanted a really nice meal, not the usual stuff made out of the van. I was done with tinned tuna, avocado and bananas. There were just five miles and a bridge to cross before we could use the public showers and spend the evening at the beach.

I found a Greek restaurant called Aegean Breeze on Google and we were both feeling that, some great comfort food. I cycled and James took the van round. Due to traffic and one-way systems I was there a little before James, so I headed into the restaurant with Brenda, which I had affectionately decided to call my bike. Brenda the bike.

"Hi," I said with a smile and walked in the front door, "I wondered if it was ok to leave my bike here." "It's ok, we can take her around the back," said a tall, olive skinned, dark haired man. "Super, I'd appreciate if it's in a safe place. I'm cycling across America and as I'm nearly there now, it would be a real shame to lose her now."

"Oh wow, yeah, it will be safer round the back, no one can access here. What you doing it for?" he asked as he took the bike from me. I followed him round.

I shared my story and we carried on chatting while he seated me at a table. By the time James arrived and sat down, my new friend, Gavin, had decided that the meal was on him. "Have whatever you like, but have the steak, please have the steak," he implored.

It was one of the greatest meals I've ever eaten, just glorious. After we'd eaten, Gavin came to clear away the plates. "So, where you heading tonight then?" he asked. "Oh, well, just heading to the beach. We're going to use the public showers down there and set up on the beach."

Gavin nodded his head with a knowing smile. "My father's holiday place is just on the beach and while there are family friends in there right now, I'm sure they won't mind you getting a shower."

Gavin was tall, classically handsome in a typical American way, and such a ray of light. There wasn't anything I could do to show how much his kindness and generosity meant to me. All I could do was say thank you and give him a hug when it was time to leave.

There is nothing quite like being at the beach as the sun sets and waking up with the sunrise. I wanted to stay there for days. The cleanliness, the white sand and blue sea is what I imagine heaven might be like.

The following days stayed like this. Blue skies and bluer seas.

On the last night of the challenge we stayed with a Warm Shower couple just 70 miles from my final destination of St Augustine. We reached the house through a forest; tall oppressive trees made navigation a challenge. Beyond the forest there were a number of houses scattered around without the usual rigid American organisation. As I approached our hosts' house, the land around it opened up slightly to reveal a two-story home with a classic America porch surrounding it. It was the stuff of movies.

There were big smiles to greet us and we got everything organised before night fell, ready for an early start the next day. The dining table was set for four in the open living area. Dinner was provided soon after we arrived. I haven't spoken much about food and hosts, but I fully accepted that you ate whatever you were given. It felt to me incredibly important that you should just fit in, unless specifically asked for a preference. There is only one food I'm really not keen on, and that's eggs. That night, the starter was a soup served with egg. I consumed it up gratefully. It is amazing what you can tolerate in the circumstances of extreme kindness and good company.

"So, which route did you do then?" asked my hosts. "Well, I didn't follow the route much," I said. "I found there were better routes, with less elevation in some places. From New Orleans I followed the coastal route because it was just more beautiful."

We continued to talk about life, cycling in America, the couple's plans for the future and also the route planned for the next day. After sharing the crazy challenges of the route, my hosts admitted that the Southern Tier Adventure cycling route had not been updated in many years. As mentioned, I had stopped following the route after New Orleans, having realised the routes weren't the best. The neglect of the Southern Tier Adventure explained so much and was glad I had given up on it.

The next day I set off before the sun had risen. I needed to be in St Augustine by 3pm. This would be a tough day of cycling, but my mindset was strong. I kept pushing on even though I wanted to stop, driven by the need to be on time and also by the bottle of fizz that I was going to consume on that beach. I was so close to being done.

I hit cycle paths for a lot of that last day, confident I would make the target. Then, quite randomly and out of nowhere I met a bull on the cycle path. I halted as smoothly as possible, spending a little time working out how I could re-route, but in the end, it involved turning back on myself. I had to reroute using the main road and then back into the cycle path. Resilience I have found, is mostly just finding a way around the bulls in life.

When I stopped to eat, a couple of stereotypical old-school Harley Davidson riders came and said hello. They were funny and encouraging, and as the sun shone, we sheltered under the shadows of a large tree. While most of the day was spent pushing on, there were moments of joy and madness, just like there had been on every other day.

As I saw the sea, a weight lifted from my shoulders. I thought about how the trace of an idea to cycle across America had turned into actually being here, completing the challenge that at times I thought I could never finish. It started as a bike, a camera, and a challenge that to so many seemed impossible, including me. Now here I was, rolling over the last bridge having started a conversation on kindness with so many incredible people.

It had not been an easy road. With some training and knowledge of bikes it would have been easier, but it wouldn't have been the life-changing journey that built up my resilience. I now understood, first-hand, that we all have the power to achieve so much, even when the people around us doubt us. This was evidenced as I hit Northern Ireland on my ElliptiGO several years later.

# Chapter 13

## ElliptiGO World Record Challenge: 2020

## "Maybe I can't do this. Maybe this is it."

I stepped into the lift, glancing at my reflection in the mirror. It looked as though someone had stuck a straw up my nostril and blown into it, so my face resembled a puffer fish. I was beyond tired and wondered how I was going to carry on. I blinked a few times, hoping that the reflection would somehow improve.

After breakfast I had to talk myself into getting up off the seat, barely able to stand let alone walk to the lift. It was 7.30am. I walked back down the corridor to my room and went back to sleep, unable to function or construct words let alone get back on Charis and travel the 40 plus miles I needed for the day.

When I woke my head felt heavy. But I had deadlines to meet, so a day off was not an option. I eventually set off at 11.30am and while the extra sleep made a huge difference, I was not firing on all cylinders.

Despite setting off late, the sun was shining and I was optimistic. I left Belfast by a continuous gradual hill for about 10 miles. This had felt unproblematic until, as I looked forwards, the gradient changed. It was more pronounced. My legs pushed hard but I kept slowing down, the physical strength leaving me.

I started to feel physically sick, and the current hill in front of me was enough of a deterrent that I simply stopped. Doubt crept in. I still had 30 miles to go and wasn't convinced I had it in me. This was different to feeling self-doubt – it was physically knowing I was potentially going to need some intervention. *Maybe I can't do this. Maybe this is it.*

Back in the empty foyer of the ferry crossing just the night before, I had set about doing social media from my phone, utilising the time as best as I could. I got up and walked over to the counter where someone had arrived to check in passengers. In a moment of lost concentration, my hand opened almost involuntarily. The phone was falling to the tiled terminal floor before I could realise what I had done. The screen immediately shattered, casting a spiderweb pattern across the glass which would have been pretty in any other circumstance. The phone was my lifeline, it had been the sat nav, podcast, map plan, emails and overall communication system for everything and everyone. It stored all the info to make the challenge possible. In my optimism I thought it would be ok. I tried to swipe my finger across the screen. Nothing happened. It was well and truly shattered. It was basically saying, "That's enough, I'm done." If I'm honest, I knew how it felt.

I had a chat with the lady at the terminal to see if someone had the special pin needed to open the sim card, and just like that she did. She also provided a hot chocolate which was the currency of kings in my opinion. I sat in the terminal, struggling to transfer everything onto the phone I used for filming. People were now boarding but I'd been told I would be last to board so we could load Charis on. Once on the ferry, and still with a broken phone, I people-watched a while. I cast my eyes over the wide-open spaces with a refreshment area visible to every person in there. Seats and tables were bolted down. TVs up on the walls displayed current news updates. The boats' noise quickly became white noise, drowned out by the mutterings of the passengers settling themselves for the nights' journey.

I observed the people around me, including a father playing with his young son, and an older man and his grown-up son in quiet and considered conversation. Lulled by the rocking of the ferry I soon laid down on the soft upholstered bench, with the reassuring smell of coffee and snacks wafting around the boat. I slept deeply and I knew I needed it. My mind was anxious for the future.

Riding through Belfast at midnight was a dream. It was cold but windless which made it pleasant. The lights and bustle were missing as I rode through the port and into the town, further evidence that lockdown was indeed ramping up.

I found the hotel that had been organised by Hilton, who had not been able to host me but arranged for me to stay somewhere else. By the time I had checked in, showered, ate, and sorted some admin, it was 2.30am. I had to be up in four hours for breakfast and to leave. I knew the mounting lethargy was about to catch up with me.

All of these circumstances led me to the point where I had to stop on the hill coming out of Belfast, seriously considering whether or not to give up.

I looked down the country road behind me, trying to figure out my options, when an attractive lady with a short blonde bob and running outfit interrupted my thoughts. As I turned to her, I realised I hadn't even heard her first words, they had simply been noise. She repeated herself, "That's an interesting bike." "Ah yes it's the ElliptiGO... I'm not sure I can get to Portrush today though, so I'm just thinking about my options." I responded.

"Hmmmm," she said, "Well, I live just half a mile up the road, so maybe you'd like to come and sit in the garden. You can have a cuppa, get some food and rest a bit." I said, "Ah, that's kind of you."

I didn't confirm or decline the offer. I just sat on the fence, not really wanting to encroach on her and her family. All my experience should have allowed me to accept her kindness promptly, but I didn't. I just wondered if I'd be able to get on the bike again. She offered a second time and I remembered the power of kindness only manifests when we accept it. So, I said yes. Her name was Hilary. Off we went up the hill, down the gravel drive and around the back of the house into the garden. "Take a seat," she said as she pointed to the wooden garden furniture. I breathed a sigh of relief. I had been holding back the tears as we walked, the sheer exhaustion taking its toll on me. Not knowing if I could achieve what I needed to came with a deep sense of grief.

I sat and spent some time breathing, simply looking out on to the garden at the lush green lawn, the flower beds around it, and trees to give privacy. Hilary popped in and out, bringing things to the table including mugs of tea. Hilary's husband arrived back from the shop with more supplies. He strolled around the corner, greeted me warmly, and Hilary shared our story of meeting. "Oh yes, I heard about your challenge on the radio. That's right, a few weeks ago," he said. We chatted some more. "Well, don't you worry, we'll get you back track one way or another," he said.

We spent the next half hour eating and chatting about how to make the day more manageable. Thinking about it still makes me well up with tears. It's difficult to put into words the profound difference their support made to the challenge and to me personally. We decided to take the bike across towards Londonderry rather than up to Portrush as was the plan. In the end, Hilary and her neighbour even rode with me.

That evening I arrived at Nicola and Sam's house. Nicola was an attractive, practical women who got on with things and her wife Sam had a depth far beyond mine and an empathy greater than most. I found them both deeply grounding.

Sam had an eye-opening intelligence. We talked for hours and I wish I had recorded all she said. She had come from New Zealand to work in England, excited to see what the world had to offer. Things had not, like in all good stories, gone to plan. She had found herself in Leeds and as she was walking down the street, she watched people hurry past homeless people, desensitised to the extreme poverty. She had come from a place where this was shocking, and she knew if she stayed, she too would also end up not caring.

This struck me then, and no doubt will continue to strike me for many years to come. How much have we desensitised ourselves to? We look at other's misfortune and find excuses for why it doesn't concern us. We turn our eyes away. What Sam said was, "I don't want to become numb and I can't save them all in this place, it's too much and too often."

I had met Nicola because she had been in touch with me a few weeks prior because of the radio interview I had done for BBC Ulster. It appeared so many people listened to the radio in Northern Ireland, which worked in my favour as a few people, including Nicola, had got in touch to offer me a place to stay. The interviewer asked me all the usual questions. It had not been any different to any other interview I'd done but it had a much more impactful response from its listeners, and I had not understood why at the time, until I learnt more about the country.

I had been reenergised and encouraged by the people I met and stayed with. However, I was still exhausted and while the love of the people had given me renewed strength, I knew a day off was needed. Charis was in need of some TLC, too. The morning sun shone and lit the sky in a dewy light and, as the morning coolness started to lift, I removed my jacket and checked the bike over knowing there was a problem with the chain. I headed to Newry next, but the chain was getting looser and I was still a phone down. If I could carry on a little further, then I might be ok. While I had not come in best physical form to Ireland, the notoriously rainy weather had held back while I was there, and this I was grateful for.

As I rode, I could see something that had died on the opposite side of the road. It was not the rabbit, fox, badger or dear that I usually saw, it was a small black ball of fur. I slowed down slightly for a moment and realised it was a black cat. About 200 yards up on the right was a house and I wondered what the best thing to do was. I wanted to get to the end as soon as possible but my conscience kicked in. Kindness is a thought process, it's not always an instant reaction. sometimes it's a weighing up of options: Is this the right thing, will the other person want this, what are all the things that will happen if I do? Equally, what will happen if I don't?

I decided people would be searching for the cat, wondering where it was, so I pulled up at the next house. It was modern and large, and as I headed to the front door, I prayed that they didn't have a cat.

I rang the doorbell, waiting for someone to answer. "Yes?" asked the man who opened the door. "Oh hello, I wondered if you had a black cat?" "Yes, we do, although we haven't seen it yet, it didn't come home last night." When I asked the simple question, I realised I had not thought through how to now provide the news that the cat might be dead. I'd set myself up to have no suitable answer that would not disturb them and seem a little callous, but honesty is usually always the kindest thing. I settled on an expression somewhere between pity and the bared teeth of Wallace from Wallace and Gromit. "I just passed a black cat in the road, I'm afraid, that's sadly dead." I felt incredibly sad for him and his family as I cycled away and wished that I had not had to share the news at all.

A little way up from the house I pulled over for some maintenance and shifted the back wheel to tighten up the chain. I travelled five more miles up and down hills to finally reach the flat cycle path that would take me into Newry.

I passed by cyclists heading the other way. As I contemplated my next move, a man popped by on my right and started chatting. I wasn't really up for company, but his presence was a huge gift I didn't realise I needed. As beautiful as the day was, I had been running out of energy and struggling in my mind. The distraction was the tonic I needed.

"So where are you heading?" "Oh, Newry. I'm heading off to Kilkenny after that and then back up the coast back to Belfast. I'm going to every city in the UK, you see." "Oh, you should definitely stop and eat at this seafood place that's just up from there on the coast. Douglas is the owner; he is a great chap." He continued to share other places to stop and eat. I wasn't quite sure that he had fully understood the whole trip, it wasn't quite the jolly that his sightseeing tips suggested. I appreciated his company though, and it passed the time. Suddenly, as if we had been transported there with no effort at all, we were at Newry, where we parted ways.

I was conscious the company of the gentleman accompanying me into Newry had given me a false sense of security regarding my ability to keep going. My energy levels were dropping. I decided I would stop, write some thank you cards and have a treat. I found a cafe and sat in the window on a high table with a stool, Charis balanced on the other side of the glass, the sun's heat warming the table. It was perfectly glorious; I had a scone with cream and a mug of hot chocolate. Have you ever eaten something in a set of circumstances that has made it the most glorious thing you have ever eaten, almost as though it's the first time you have tasted it? That is what this was like.

"Is that your bike out there?" A lady with short dark hair and fair skin asked me. "Oh yes, that's mine. I'm doing a World Record on it and headed through every city in the UK. Actually, it would be wonderful if you could sign my book to be a witness." "Yes, of course love. Are you doing it for charity?" I explained the mission again as though it was the first time while she took my book and signed. Her face lit up and she had been enthralled and enthusiastic about it, so much so that she had gifted me my food. I wrote an extra thank you card and eventually peeled myself away from the warmth of the window and set off on my way.

I headed down the hard shoulder of the motorway along with tractors and other cyclists, sticking to the coastline towards Kilkeel to make the most of this flat section of the road. That afternoon the wind picked up and I soon lost the energy gained from the perfect cream tea. The sea views were stunning, and I felt so close to my rest day, to having space and sleeping in, but even as I got ever closer, I felt like I would never get there. When we stand in an incredibly challenging moment, the place we are trying to seek often seems like a mirage. I couldn't imagine ever getting the amount of rest that my body so badly needed.

I came off the main road, still hugging the coastline. I tackled the first major hill, knowing it would be easier once this main part was under my belt. I was nearly at the top when I turned and looked out over the sea to see a picture perfect, postcard view. It forced me to stop.

"What is this life, if full of care, we have no time to stop and stare?" I told myself.

In my desperation to reach my destination, I was spending so much of my time begging the future to come. So, I knew I had to appreciate these moments or every second, minute and hour of the trip would pass me by. The view was outstanding, the sea, the falling sun, the cove full of bobbing boats. I don't know how long I stood there. Maybe no amount of time would have been enough.

I was on a country road, and behind me a lady was stood behind a low stone wall. "Terrible view you have here," I said. The lady responded, "Yes, we really hate it." After chatting to her some more I carried on. The downhills from the previous climbs greeted me like an old friend, helping me onwards in my race against the sun.

A few miles of dangerous road later, I was on a straight and due to turn right with only five miles left to cycle. The headwind had whipped itself into a fury and would be against me as I turned the corner. To my right, a car was parked in a lay-by, the driver waving at me to stop. As she got out of her car, my fear kicked in and every detective book I had ever read came flooding back, reminding me of a thousand ways I could be in danger. A second later I saw her face and recognised her as the lady I had spoken to over the wall.

I crossed the road as she helped a small painfully shy boy of about eight get out of the back of the car. "We wanted to bring you something to help you on your way. Wow, though, you came much further than we thought you would have! We thought we might have missed you. I hope you don't mind. We bought you tea, cookies and sweets." "No of course not, this is wonderful!" "My husband will think I've gone mad when I tell him about what I've done. My sister already thought I was mad when I told her. But I knew, after meeting you and hearing your story, if I didn't bring you something, I'd regret it, you know what I mean?"

And there it was. A moment in time allowing me to understand the importance of sharing our stories. They provide inspiration and power to those who care to listen. There is something really wonderful about when someone is vulnerable and truly honest and pushes the boundaries of their own comfort.

"Would it be ok to get a photo?" asked the lady. "We can share it for my son's show and tell at school." The boy stood near me and Charis as we smiled brightly for the photo. I pulled out a thank you card from my bike bags and wrote out, "Thank you so much for the treats, I had been really struggling these past few days and your kindness has given me the strength to power through today."

When they left, I sipped my tea from the paper cup and ate the cookies. The sun was still setting, and time was ticking but suddenly I was in no rush, as though time did not exist. Chatting with the lady and her son had been an energising pleasure and reminded me that some things were more important than meeting deadlines. I looked out at the sea, everything level with my eye line. The tide was out, and light reflected on the wet, rippled sand.

I had been forced to stop and enjoy the moment, and I was grateful. Beyond the gift of conversation and the tea and treats, the woman and her sweet son had given me the ability to live in that particular moment, to have taken a picture in my mind's eye of that stunning view. It was the greatest gift they could have given me.

The last five miles riding against a strong headwind felt like nothing, I didn't care that it was taking twice as long as it should have, or that it was cooling down as the sun set. Connection in the form of kindness really is one of the most powerful motivators.

There were often a couple of cathedrals in each Irish cities, one Roman Catholic and one Church of Ireland. The church of Ireland is Protestant and represents England heritage. The majority of Irish people are Roman Catholic. War and loss of life has ravaged Northern Ireland. There are books that explain the lifetime of destruction between opposing groups, so I won't try to explain the long and complicated history here. I picked up stories from people I met, feeling the grief that ran deep within them from the death of loved ones and the blood of people they didn't know that ran in the streets. Fear had risen up during the conflict and caused some to attack, but it also led to a deep sense of empathy and an understanding that life does not grow without kindness.

It had been an extreme ride in Ireland, and I'd had to rely on people more than at any other part of the trip. When I was there, I got the feeling that the grief and bloodshed had produced a superior society. It seemed that each Irish person I met was able to see that wars did not make change. They knew that it was simply each individual action that they took to support one another that would create change. They understood loud and clear that society changes with each individual deciding to make it so.

I don't know which cathedrals I went to. To me, it didn't matter. If each individual chooses to see past the divides, eventually we can truly come together.

I was now safely at the Shepherds hut I was staying at with the lovely Liam and Alice on the coast. They had sent help to resolve the issues with Charis. That help arrived in an old-style land rover. The driver was Cyril, a friendly guy with a strong Irish lilt. "Are you the lady with the funny bike?" he asked. I laughed. "Yes, I am. The bikes under the shelter there."

Cyril knelt down, immediately figuring out how the bike worked. There was quickly a black smear of oil on his nose from the chain. He was the sort of person who would simply make the tools he needed rather than buy them, and his workshop, he said, was bigger than his house. A handy person to have in a town, I imagine.

We chatted over the bike, and I could tell that he didn't really understand the purpose of what I was doing. Some people didn't get it, it was just the way of things sometimes. But as I spoke to him, overlooking the Irish countryside, he said something I'll never forget.

"I've been to London once to visit a friend," he told me. "I'll be honest, I don't understand it. The houses prices, for a start. You spend hours at work, you have no time, and have to buy your meals ready made. Then you have to start all over again to pay for the expensive house you've bought." His viewpoint was valuable and simple, and a stark reminder of our need for fast lives, ultimately feeding the fast-food epidemic and leading to poor nutrition. "The secret is to know that each of us are completely different. When we understand that and accept that, everything is easier," he said.

And there we have it. In one sentence, the answer to so many of the challenges that face humanity. You can fix any issue of hate or disagreement simply by getting people to understand and accept that nobody is, or should be, the same. A good reminder as I moved onto my next challenge.

# Chapter 14

## Walking 500 miles: 2019

## "Whose blooming idea was this!"

My faithful old walking boots sank into the ground with every step I took. I had not come far and the road ahead felt impossibly far away. I'd already taken so many wrong turns following the coast but was energised by the sea and the unseasonal sunshine. As I kept going, I asked myself, *Can I even do this? Is it possible? Where will I sleep tonight?*

My legs felt the pressure as I continued to push on, the crunching of my steps complimenting the rhythmic steady waves, a sound I know I will never tire of. I lifted my head and for miles all I could see was a sea of tiny pebbles. The ocean was quiet, as if like me it was considering itself and its options.

This year, my choice of challenge had come down to resources. I had no money left to do any other sort of challenge and walking seemed physically easy and, to an extent, free. I'd done very little training; I know you'll be shocked to hear that revelation!

So, why did I choose to walk 500 miles, and how did I go about planning it? Well, I had decided to take it easy on myself (I write this with a smile on my face of course). I planned to start somewhere near my home in the south of England, and end at the top England. 500 miles seemed a long enough distance to get some media coverage about kindness but not so impossible that I couldn't achieve it. It also had a great ring to it, 'I will walk 500 miles,' in line with the old Pretenders' song… but I won't walk 500 more!

However as is often the case, my optimism meant that I underestimated the challenge. Walking, I discovered, is considerably harder than you might imagine. But there is something about going in with little knowledge that can work in your favour. You learn to figure it out as you go, and if you had all the information at the start you probably wouldn't even try. I believe this is called 'blind optimism', and I for one am very good at it.

I was going to be relying on staying with friends along the way, which was another sign of my innate faith in the world. It's difficult to describe, but I guess I always believe that everything works out in the end. Paul used to describe me as having 'more jam than Hartley's', as this innate faith meant that things tended to work out for me in the end. Even when things don't go to plan, I know that what you put into the world will in the end come back to help you along when the chips are down.

My original plan was to walk from school to school in a seamless sequence of talks and workshops on the topic of kindness. The days spent planning and chasing support were endless. I worked out a rough route of counties I would pass through between Swanage and Gretna Green, then found a list of schools to email. I explained I would come to the school and deliver a talk and a kindness workshop, all for free. I can still remember the moment I pressed send, thinking, "Well, 700 schools contacted, that's a good job done! I'll wait for the responses and work out the route from there." I waited and waited and in total received four responses back.

I phoned the schools from the list; in my optimism I believed they had just not received the email. The schools gave little back. The decision makers and support staff wouldn't give me an answer either way. No one wanted to say no, but few people said yes. At the time I couldn't understand why there wasn't more interest. "I'm giving my time to share a cool story with your students, a free workshop on kindness, and help your school join a movement to promote kindness. What's not to like?" However, I was blind to the internal challenges within schools to find the time and resources to set up anything outside of the curriculum. It wasn't just the schools that had been unresponsive. I sat at the dining room table, my laptop lighting up my face. Darkness had come with no warning. I ran through my digital to do list, sending a call-out to ask people to consider the power of kindness rather than money. I'd write to organisations that might be able to give support, and I'd contact media agents for publicity. It was about trying to change the dominant narrative that life and success are measured by money. The message was always the same.

I want to take a moment here to touch on the relentless PR that needs to happen to promote a message. Using the media is far from an ego-driven self-promotion. This could not be further from the truth. Trust me, if someone else could give the message and someone else wanted to do a challenge for kindness, I could promote them much better than I can promote myself. I'm always holding back, never really wanting to be in the limelight, but knowing it's the only way to get the message out there, a message that I am passionate about. My personal story is compelling and for many it inspires them to live their best lives. I started completing annual challenges to start a conversation about kindness being worth more than money. These adventures are a way to promote the power kindness can have to save lives and transform society. I often wonder, though, why the conversation on kindness is not more credibly snapped up by the media.

For example, I can remember a chap sat on the red sofa of our local news programme and spoke about his challenge to go through all the American states by bike. He was doing it to raise money for anti-bullying charities. It was the same TV channel I had chased and sent several emails to about my challenge promoting kindness but had no luck. Sadly, there is a real desire to dwell on the negative within life and media.

Fast forward to my 500-mile walk, and I lay in bed, throbbing coming from various parts of my body. I had been prescribed rest, despite barely starting the many miles ahead. There was much sucking through teeth as people advised me that maybe I should quit. I could hear the voices now, well-meaning but negative all the same. "I don't know how you will do this." "Bit silly to continue now." "This is too much for you." However, I had learnt that if you let the voices and fears of others enter your mind, you've only got yourself to blame when you don't do what you say you will.

Just two weeks before I walked along the beach at the start of my 500-mile challenge, I had badly damaged my finger in a netball match. It was bearable, but the weight of the bag on my shoulder along with the blood flow from my hand while walking was exacerbating the pain. I had also picked up a niggling pain in my knee. I was not a seasoned adventurer; if I had been, I'm sure I would have stopped or done something better than just carry on. There is a fine line between pushing on and pushing too hard. My determination to carry on meant that I had to take four days of rest while my knee recovered.

I was soon on my way again, with my knee tightly wrapped in a support. I could feel the binding ease the pain, but it was consistent and relentless all the same. As I moved into the county of Somerset, the green pastures and unseasonal balmy weather was enough to keep me trudging on. In the end, after many phone calls and cajoling over the past few months, I was due to visit 10 schools. When I approached my second school to complete a set of assemblies, a teacher had offered to put me up in his family home. His name was Steve and he was as jolly a teacher as you could hope to have. I left their school in the afternoon after doing three assemblies and a kindness workshop and headed to their home. It was a six-hour walk and at the end the darkness was blinding, no moon or streetlights to illuminate the country roads. Scratches from furrowing animals and mournful owl cries set the hairs on my arms on end. The cold had no impact, I was walking fast, powered by the need to reach my destination. However, for the last few miles Steve came and joined me, and it was a joy to have company. The rhythmic chit-chat meant that the time passed by quicker. I walked into the village that was our final end point. It felt familiar, as though I had spent time there when I was a child and the memories had not fully formed.

In front of me, our shadows swept across the road, now lit up by dim streetlights. Steve passed me an apple. "Wasn't sure what would be good, so I bought apples." It was a seemingly small act, but it was a thought that felt so much bigger. When you have nothing, any tiny act of kindness matters. Steve had left his home thinking; *I wonder what I can do to support this lady when I meet her? What will she need? What would I need?* He put himself in my shoes. The apple was the end result of a sequence of kindness values that passed through the core of him. Empathy, I have learnt, is the greatest way to connect with each other through the challenges of the world we live in.

We arrived at Steve's house and his wife and grown up children welcomed me into their home. We all sat and ate dinner together. The house was a beautiful large cottage that had been carefully restored with modern décor.

"So, tell us about your challenges," Steve asked, hopeful maybe that I would be able to share the story of resilience and inspire his family in the same way I had inspired the students at the school. I did my best, although my message is more powerful when I can pace a school hall and share a video on a big screen. Dinner time doesn't lend itself to such moments, and I felt that maybe I didn't deliver it with quite the same gusto.

I was back on the road before long. For the end of the winter, the weather was warm. The sun had mostly been on my side. I was able to post updates on my social media pages with ease, and while I had physical pain trying to halt me, I was still pushing on.

I shared the route I would take on social media. However, in reality I would need to make detours to avoid hills and especially busy roads. It then came as a surprise and a huge disappointment to me when a supporter had left a lovely care package for me, displaying the Sunshine People logo and my name, along with a message of support. Due to a detour, I didn't pass the place where they had left the package, but the thought behind it impacted me hugely. I always think it's just my mother and on occasion my friends that watch or follow my kindness message. But it's the people who pop up and show me there is some impact being made in the world that gives me hope that what I am doing makes a difference, however small it might be. All that thought, all that time, all that meaning, in one little package. It was a joy when everything at the time hurt from so much walking. It gave me hope that the walk mattered.

The weather held out. Although I'd expected it to be freezing cold, we were seeing a balmy February which was a blessing. *You've got more jam than Hartley's, Summers,* continued to ring in my ears.

In the south of England, I had enough contacts to keep me going for places to stay and eat, but north of Birmingham it was looking a little bleak because on the route I was taking I knew very few people.

When I booked in a talk at each school, I would also ask if there were any teachers who would be happy to put me up. It was one of the highlights of the trip, meeting people I didn't know, hearing their stories and seeing how they live their lives. It was not only fascinating but completely humbling that people would allow me into their homes and share their history with me. There really is no greater honour.

As I arrived in Bath a sprinkling of showers had started. The weather was on the turn and my jam was starting to run out. It was a timely reminder to consider getting some waterproof trousers and some sort of shoe coverings but, before I did that, I needed to deliver a talk at the local girls' school. I wasn't sure of the way and so followed the maps on my phone. It dawned on me as I walked, a feeling that rose up from my feet spreading across my body all the way to my head, that I was walking the same road that Paul had died on. The memories of that fateful day were creeping upon me. I could feel the same hopeless, heart wrenching distress as he told me he thought he was having a heart attack, and then died alone at that spot on the busy road.

It had not dawned on me until I looked along the road. I kept walking, although every part of my body wanted to stop, to allow myself to accept the moment. I knew if I was going to deliver the talk, I had to keep walking. A feeling of energy swam through my body, something that was not unpleasant but had an air of longing to it, for a time gone by and all that could and should have been. I continued to walk. When I passed the place where Paul had taken his final breath, I left a little part of me there on the tarmac, even after all this time when I thought I had already given so much. Tears rolled down my face and my heart lifted and fell in the passing moments as I continued to walk. An hour later I stood in front of 600 people and delivered a talk about the power of kindness with my whole heart and truth. Kindness had truly seen me out of the darkness and into the light.

I had very little funds, so had to consider carefully what to do about the creeping cold. Maybe plastic bags on my feet would do, if I used what money I had to buy some waterproof trousers? I needed to not be wasteful, using something just for this challenge then never again sat heavily with me. Reusing and borrowing items seemed more practical and better for the environment, but I had not got this organised before I left.

After I finished at the school, I headed back into Bath city centre. I went into three outdoors shops. The first two were large chain stores, with surprisingly limited stock and slightly dismissive staff. The last of the three was my saviour, BCH Camping, a small privately-owned shop which didn't look like much on the outside, but it was full of wisdom and light in the dark.

"Hi, can I help you?" A pretty girl offered as I walked to the back of the shop. "Well, I am doing a 500-mile walk and while I've been blessed with good weather, I think it may be on the turn," I explained. "I'm pretty limited by funds but need to get something to keep my feet dry, and some waterproof trousers if possible." The girl frowned in thought for a moment. "Well," she said, "We have these waterproof socks." "Oh, they seem like a great solution," I said, picking them up off the rack.

Chris, another assistant, joined in the conversation after finishing up with a customer. We chatted about the challenge.

Chris was an Expedition Leader and knew a lot, so he started to help me plan the next part of my route. I must have stayed at the shop for an hour chatting with them both, in which time Chris had bought out some used waterproof trousers that I could have from his personal stash of equipment. I bought the socks and off I went, knowing that the connections I had made had brought me out of the emotional place I had found myself in earlier that morning.

# Chapter 15

## ElliptiGO World Record Challenge: 2020

## "Look at her legs man!"

I was on the cycle path from Glasgow to Prestwick, 15 miles of gradual incline followed by 15 more miles downhill. It was due to rain late in the afternoon, so I set off at first light in freezing fog.

I pushed on as the freezing fog was replaced by sleet. It gave no rest and when I arrived at the Hilton Hotel in Glasgow, I stood dripping in the entrance not quite knowing how to get myself and Charis in without causing a terrible mess. The customer service manager came to my rescue, taking my clothes to the laundrette and giving me the thickest, fluffiest dressing gown I have ever worn. I ran a bath, put something easy to watch on my laptop and sipped some complementary fizz. Sinking into the hot bubbly water was the most wonderful self-indulgence, allowing me to forget for a moment about the pressure, the pain and the steadily growing lump in my breast.

The lump was now visible through my t-shirts. I knew I had to do something about it soon, but I had momentum and the thought of stopping seemed impossible. People often believe that it is Paul's memory driving me on, which of course used to be true. But what first started me on this path is not my motivation now. What keeps me focused today is the need for real, lasting change in society where trust, integrity, connection and empathy are at the forefront of our actions.

I am not an 'excuses' person, I would rather work to find a solution. If I wanted to quit something, I would quit because I didn't want to do it anymore, not because some external factor hindered its success. This time though, there were so many other pandemic-related factors coming into play. Due to COVID-19, discussions were in place to close all hotels – a sure sign I would need to pause my trip.

There were more practical problems slowing me down, too. The bike's chains were worn and a bike shop 1,000 miles back on the journey had advised replacing the main cogs. I finally booked Charis in to see Martin at Roots, a cycle shop up in Dunblane, on my day off. The morning came and went with the parts only arriving at 1pm, forcing me to add a second unscheduled day off while they were fitted.

There was something thick in the air, a feeling of unease that enveloped me and made my skin crawl. It was based on not knowing if my next decision would be the right one, but also something else that I couldn't put my finger on. It wasn't pleasant.

I was about 3,500 miles in to the total 5,000 miles of the journey. Not only was I navigating the UK, I was also swerving around the constant uninvited hurdles that kept popping up. My mind was drawn to all the work and the people who were invested in the success of the challenge. Stopping didn't seem like an option, but it also felt like a year and a half of work was set to fall down flat.

Whenever I am in doubt, I reach out to others for support. That evening, I made a call to my old friend Scott. He is one of those people everyone likes, always a laugh, always open and always kind. He has been my go-to person through all of my major challenges, and when I'm at the bottom, he seems to pull me back up with incredible grace.

After a few pleasantries he asked me how I was feeling about the challenge. I took a deep breath. "I just feel like I'm not sure if I should be carrying on," I said, "Is it worth it? My health is not great, and my energy levels are rapidly declining."

I shared how I had felt in Ireland – so run down and exhausted – and explained how I had to rely on a large amount of support from other people to get me through. Scott made encouraging sounds while I spoke, to reassure me and let me know he was listening. "I mean, I think my mindset is just not in the place to power me through," I finished.

After a short pause, Scott said, "There are a few things here. I think, firstly, we need to consider a vitamin programme to help with your physical energy. Your body has depleted over the past few months and you need a boost." He proceeded to recommend a vitamin programme, ordering them for me to pick up the next day as I cycled through Perth. Well, that might be one problem solved.

"Ok, so what about mindset?" I asked. "I just don't know if what I'm doing is right. Am I just a silly woman on a bike trying to start a conversation that no-one cares about? It's getting more and more difficult and every other day I deal with major hurdles and problems and I really don't know if I have it in me to deal with anymore. Nothing about this challenge has been easy and I wonder if someone is trying to tell me something and I'm too stubborn to hear them."

"Mmmm," pondered Scott. "Have you drawn back to remember why you are doing this? Do you still have the purpose in your heart? Remind yourself of your reason and draw on that."

I was stunned. It was so simple. I had been overcomplicating things, when really what I needed was to be single-minded and practical about what I wanted to achieve, why, and how I was going to do it. Scott pulled my mindset back, helping me work out tangible actions to distract from the mental blocks and negative thoughts like listening to podcasts. I'd promised myself I would do that throughout the challenge, and try to learn new things along the way, but somewhere, somehow, I'd lost my way on the road.

My conversation with Scott focused my mind. I was able to draw back to my purpose: to plant seeds in the world that will be watered by others, taking positive actions that continue to ripple out. Most of the time, I don't hear about the acts of kindness that my story inspires. So yes, of course I should continue, even if I never get to see what happens as a result. My talk with Scott helped me see life doesn't get any easier. I'd keep jumping hurdles for the rest of the challenge, but I would build my resilience, and that was in itself a great gift.

Over the next four days I travelled up the east coast of Scotland, a section I had looked forward to. Charis was in the best health possible; the wind was behind me and I had a new plan. I decided to keep my mind occupied, focusing less on the overall challenge and more on distraction. I listened to the 'Tough Girls' podcast, a selection of interviews conducted by Sarah Williams of inspiring and adventurous women. It was just what the doctor ordered.

I stopped to restock on food coming into Perth. As I loaded the provisions into my bags outside the supermarket, a man approached me.

"Oh, what's this then? Where you headed?"

I told him my story I had told a thousand times with the same level of enthusiasm as the first time I had been asked. As I finished my elevator pitch, another man approached having caught the back end of the story. "So, is it electric?" the second man asked.

Quick as a flash, the first man, very offended on my behalf, said, "Of course it's not, look at her legs, man!"

It was the best compliment, although some may not have appreciated it. For the first time I considered the fitness I had gained. I spent most of my time moaning about pain or discomfort, so to gain a healthy side effect was a welcome bonus.

Freewheeling down carless roads, I barely had to work. Charis being newly serviced also helped. The Scottish cathedrals were far more modest than those I'd seen before, but they had a certain charm and I took pictures as evidence of visiting them all the same.

Up the east coast of Scotland, the views were other worldly. Somewhere along the coast – it doesn't really matter exactly where – I set off from a small town between Aberdeen and Perth. It was early morning when I began the day's cycle, revelling in the cool air and crispness that wakes you like a kiss, energising you for the day ahead. I left the town boundaries and hit the coastline. As the skyline opened up, the fragmented clouds formed the pattern of a leopard's spots, with the rising sun beaming through the gaps. It was a sunrise I will never forget.

A lady passed by me while I took a moment to appreciate the beauty. She was apologising profusely as she walked past, as she had not been able to figure out how to stop Dolly Parton's 'Working 9-5' blaring from her phone. As she walked away, I set off again, popping the song onto my playlist as I cruised up the coast, enjoying the unique and stunning scenery.

I started to really see things again, appreciating what was around me. However, the days were very quickly getting shorter, and I was not getting any faster. I recognised this might cause a problem later down the road.

As you know, the UK's endless hills were a challenge and in Scotland there was no let up. But something was shifting within me. Now, as I approached each hill, I thought, "Well, I'll just go as far as I can and then I'll stop when I need to." It was because of this kindness to myself, this conscious act of telling myself it was ok if I didn't make it, that I found myself powering through regardless.

Immediately after leaving Aberdeen I ended up on a dual carriageway A-road with no hard shoulder. An impending doom washed over me. My body was on high alert, trying to find a way through, a deer caught in the headlights with no break in the hedge to disappear into. There was no way back and no way around. My body stopped. It was telling me to think, find a solution, don't rush this. I got up onto the wide grass verge. Cars were whizzing by, and as I recorded a short video to share my predicament to those who followed the adventure, a lorry went by so fast it nearly dragged me into the road.

I knew my thinking time was up. I started to walk without much thought at all. I stuck to the grass verge, as far from the hurtling traffic as possible. Pushing Charis and all my kit up the steep hill was uncomfortable, but a survival instinct had kicked in. Something was pushing me on that I can't explain. I had to keep stopping to ease the discomfort in my legs and arms for a moment before continuing. I could see from the map on my phone that there was a left turn up ahead that would lead me away from the A-road. It would add miles to the journey, but at this stage it was the safest thing to do.

Turning left onto the small backroad with tall trees on either side was paradise compared to the extremity of the road I had escaped. Suddenly the hills I was going up didn't seem so bad, and I overlooked the deserted country roads and vast Scottish land with a sense of relief. However, soon I was left with no choice but to head back onto the A9 again. It was not as brutal, but it was still gut churning. As I came around and down a hill, I spotted a petrol station in the valley like a most welcome mirage. I took a slow, measured breath for the first time in a while, stopping at the garage to gain some confidence. I also wanted to ask for some advice as to how I might make the last miles easier. Was there a route I didn't know about, that didn't show on the map, that only the locals knew?

I parked Charis and walked up to the two ladies working behind the counter. "Hi, I'm wondering if there's a way to get me off this road. I'm heading to Keith."

"'Fraid not," came the response, in a deep Scottish accent. "It gets easier though, once you get up over this hill here. It no' as hilly."

Impressed by my venture, the women signed my evidence book and offered me a hot chocolate which I accepted without a second thought. The weather was cold, and I was uneasy. I didn't know how much I had needed comfort and kindness, which they gave in spades. I headed back on the road with the positive message that while there was a hill yet to come, afterwards it would be easy going.

Something I've learnt not only during the challenges but in life in general is to always expect people to do the unexpected. It doesn't matter how prepared you are – other people are unpredictable. As I was approaching Keith, I was reminded of this once again.

I'd got into the habit of eyeing drivers to make sure they had clocked me as I approach their vehicles. This simple tactic had kept me safe throughout all of the challenges I'd done to date. For the 3,026 miles of the ElliptiGO challenge, this system had managed to keep me off any car bonnets.

A truck on my left was about to pull out from a junction, turning in the same direction as me. I tried to make eye contact, but this time the driver was not paying attention. I could see from the blankness of his eyes that his mind was elsewhere, so I was poised to swerve as I approached. Predictably unpredictable, he cut across me and I was able to react quickly and go wide. My heart raced, adrenaline fuelling my entire body. Heat coursed from my pounding chest to the very tips of my fingers, a contrast to the coolness in the air. I had spent the day on my wits and this close encounter did nothing to dampen the flames.

I continued on and did not react to the driver. I had nothing left to give. Then, to my right, the driver slowed level with me, his passenger window open. "I am so sorry, it was totally my fault, I didn't see you there, I really am so sorry!"

The apology came from the heart; I could see from his face that he was mortified by what could have so easily happened had I not reacted quickly. Anger had no place in my already spent body, only extreme empathy. How would I feel if I were in his shoes? I would feel terrible, shaken and a little scared. He did not need me pointing out what he already knew, so I simply said, "It's ok, don't worry."

In the UK, there was more talk of lockdowns and a tier system where certain areas would face greater restrictions to halt the spread of COVID-19. I needed to get out of Scotland and back into England, fast. I was always weighing up my options, always working out a plan B, C and D for every scenario. It had been a rollercoaster of a day; my energy dipping in and out. I tried to adapt as best I could, changing the route as I encountered obstacles in real time.

I headed down cycle paths as much as I could, adding miles to the journey to ensure I stayed on the country roads and kept away from people and built-up areas. There was beauty on the ride, tree-lined country roads and wide shallow rivers with wooden bridges that were almost timeless. For the most part I just tried to push through, my mind focused on making it to Inverness. I had an extreme pain in my big toes that was making riding almost impossible, but I'd handled pain in so many forms that I kept going regardless.

While I sought out the deserted back roads, sometimes larger roads were unavoidable. I just kept peddling. If you think too much about anything, you can make the situation more dangerous than is necessary.

I had been plagued with injuries, health issues, changes in the plan, finding places to stay, food, exhaustion, COVID regulations, and how it all effected the trip. I re-planned as I went along, keeping my own business going. There were a thousand reasons to stop, but I asked my future self, "Would you be happy if you stopped?" The answer was always no, no I wouldn't.

I had been on the road for two and a half months. I'd come to think of myself as a machine, one that needed a lot of servicing and tended to break down a lot, but a machine all the same. Waking up in Inverness, I fuelled my body for the day ahead. Then, like a clock reaching its set time, an internal alarm went off. It hit me like a thunderbolt. I was in the last city of my journey; the most northerly city I would encounter. It meant, ultimately, that I was heading home. While it would take me six weeks, this realisation made my heart sing more than any other I had had on the trip. It was so exciting. I was going home! I wasn't going to quit just because it got tough, but I was only going to continue if it was safe and legal. My desire to stop and be finished did not factor. I hadn't come this far to just come this far.

173

To start with, the 36 miles to Aviemore were brutal. Hills punctuated the first five miles out of Inverness, but the views were out of this world. Once I had tackled those first five miles, the hills eased, and the wind settled. Overnight, the trees seemed to have turned to every possible shade of autumn. It was impossible not to see the beauty, despite the pain in my feet and the tiredness in my bones. There is something about the changing colours of the seasons that reaches into your soul and shakes you. I wanted the bronze, copper and golds to soak into my very being.

In the shadow of ever changing COVID regulations, I often worried about how I might keep going. I could stay at hotels, but I couldn't stay in people's homes anymore. I still had 40 days to go and staying in a hotel each night was just not feasible. I had one gifted night and a couple of Hilton stays left, but with the changing weather, lack of accommodation could be a deal breaker. Suddenly, a sense that it would be ok washed over me.

That day, as I pondered upon some solutions and wondered if I could carry a tent on Charis, I got an email from the chair of Rotary in the north. The chair had been due to host me along the way but were now unable to because of COVID. The email went on to explain that Rotary had some unused funds due to COVID that had not been needed for travel and events. It would buy me at least six nights of hotel stays when I was in the cities, perhaps a few more if I could find cheap places to stay. Just like that, I was breathing again. I didn't even know I was holding my breath throughout these times of uncertainty.

Whenever I thought, *maybe this is it, maybe I can't go on, maybe this is the thing that will force me to stop*, I'd be given a message that would make me understand that I had to go on. I was still stuck for many parts of the final leg of the challenge, but thanks to my Rotary hosts I had another week of respite before I had to worry again. So, I kept going.

Although I was homeward bound, the roads and the difficulties they threw at me were no more forgiving. The day I damaged my wrist was especially tough. The morning rain was relentless, coming down in sheets, but it was due to clear by the afternoon. I knew a day riding in the rain could be dangerous and in a desperate attempt to avoid it I delayed setting off until 1.30pm, leaving just five hours before sunset.

I was on a mission. I needed to follow the schedule, to do what I had committed to do. I could not take it easy and would have no time to stop along the way. I used my gears a lot to keep pushing on at the maximum speed while reserving my energy levels as much as possible.

I got my head in the game using every trick I'd learnt. I repeated mantras. I played a constant stream of uplifting, motivating music in one ear, listening out for traffic with the other. I broke down my goal into bitesize chunks. "I've just got to go 10 miles; can I do that," I told myself. I counted to four over and over again, which became a form of meditation. I thought about stories, worked out hopes and dreams, made plans for what my life would one day look like, pushing down on those pedals harder and faster all the while.

I was in the zone. I didn't notice the pain building, too desperate to make the end point. The next day, when I got on the bike, the stabbing ache in my wrist made my face contort and my eyes water. The machine was broken, but something was saying, "Just keep going, we'll fix you while you go." It was like pushing a car with punctured tyres.

I stopped at a pharmacy at a small tourist town and they applied pain relieving gel and provided me with a wrist support. It didn't scratch the surface of the pain. My riding became more mindful. I was aware of every hill I approached, and every gear change required. I knew if I didn't use my wrist for a few days it would no doubt get better, but I was on my way home now. Nothing was getting in my way.

# Chapter 16

## Walking 500 miles: 2019

## "Stop Henry; it's the lady from the TV!"

On my 500-mile walk across the UK, the picturesque city of Oxford would be my longest stopping point. I had arranged to work with a school for three days, hosting a number of assemblies and workshops. A teacher had agreed to put me up in their spare room and arriving at the house was a welcome relief. Dropping my bag, I felt literally and figuratively lighter.

Waking up the next day, the miles had taken their toll. I was both physically and mentally exhausted and ended up spending most of the day recovering in bed. I made the most of the time off by catching up on admin and planning the next stages of my route, removing the anxiety that had been building up.

As I lay in bed, thinking about the future of my challenge, I realised that in less than a week I was unlikely to have anywhere to sleep. The lack of places to stay beyond Birmingham was a problem I could no longer ignore. With a certain amount of trepidation, I uploaded a post on my Facebook page. Strongly believing things will 'all work out in the end' and actively pushing towards that outcome is vital not only for contained challenges but also for our lives in general. It has saved me, numerous times, from dipping into a place that I might mentally struggle to escape from.

The next morning after my day of relative rest, I got dressed and headed on the short walk to the school. It was bright but the winter cold still struck my face, the coolness contrasting to the warmth of my body that was wrapped up in my walking gear. I sat in the school's reception areas waiting to be collected by a teacher, looking at the artwork that adorned the walls and listening to the snippets of conversation and arrangements being made to solve the days' challenges.

After being greeted by the teacher, I was led to a large hall where a few hundred children sat. The video explaining my challenge was already up on the wall. Standing in front of them, I told them the powerful story of how 10 minutes of kindness can change not only an individual's life but the entire world.

After the assembly, I held an hour-long workshop with a group of 12 of the school's most 'difficult' students to try to motivate them to be kinder. To keep them engaged, I added in lots of interactive games. In one of the games, someone could stand up and say all the mean things they could think of to another person, and the 'victim' could only react in a non-confrontational way, for example, saying "I don't mind," or "I agree with you."

I picked a particularly boisterous girl to do the exercise with me. She began insulting me and all of the other kids began to laugh. After the game, she walked up to me gingerly and whispered, "I want you to know that I don't mean any of those things I said, and I really like what you do."

And there we have it, maybe all the confirmation I ever needed. It told me so much about who she was. The girl was not saying this to me for the sake of it, she was saying it because it was what she believed. She, while seen as less kind than her peers who were not involved in the workshop, was in fact demonstrating the epitome of kindness by providing reassurance and going out of her way to do so. Kindness is within us all, but things happen in life which makes it harder to be vulnerable enough to show it.

I'd not been able to gain any press coverage in Oxford and had received what was essentially a very dismissive 'F-off' from them, which was mirrored in the passers-by I met. As I went up the path, I said hello or simply smiled at everyone I passed. No-one responded. I shrugged it off and kept moving forwards.

I checked the responses to my Facebook post when I got back to my host's house. The post had been shared hundreds of times with comments from people who could offer support. I planned out the places I would stay as far I was able to, sleeping a little easier that night knowing I wasn't alone in my battle and a whole tribe of people wanted to promote kindness over money.

The following day, I was due to meet an old school friend in Oxford town centre, which meant walking back along the canal. It was drizzling as I greeted my friend. A 24-mile day lay ahead of us like impending doom, but her company enveloped me like a blanket. As we walked, conversation took us from our school days to where we were now, and the future of the world as a whole. We chatted with ease as we moved along the contours of the paths. As we neared the last few miles, we were both struggling to keep going, but I knew from experience we would finish strong because we were doing it together.

The daffodils had started to bloom on the verges as I continued to walk down the country roads. More of the little yellow trumpets were emerging each day, fighting through the cold hard soil.

The Birmingham canal paths were a real gift – straight and direct. This gave me time to think without worrying about heading off on the wrong path. The beauty of the still waters and the sun shining through the trees was inspiring, and I started calling friends to hash out the ideas that swam in my mind.

I relentlessly pestered the BBC Midlands news desk in the hope that the 500-mile challenge would be covered. Press and media are always a challenge. I did too many radio interviews to mention and a number of TV interviews, but for me it was never enough. How do I change the narrative that we continue to live by? How do I encourage people to see the inherent flaws in measuring success by money? Why do we keep striving for more of something that doesn't bring us true happiness? I wrote to media stations and kept chasing until someone responded. It was hard work and I realised I needed to start asking myself some all-important questions: what did I hope would happen if I was featured, and how did I expect the world to change as a result? If I'm honest, I wasn't sure I knew the answers. I was blindly pushing forwards, hoping something would stick, and maybe for now that was enough.

Eventually my perseverance with BBC Midlands paid off. They needed a positive story as the whole news day had been 'doom and gloom'. Due to familiarity, and because I care very little about what people think about me, I'm relatively unfazed by interviews. I neither look forward to them or feel unnerved by them. My message is so simple: recognise and promote the power of kindness in society. However, sitting on the red sofa with the legendary Nick Owen was surreal. I grew up watching him on TV and suddenly, sat in clothes I'd spent the last three weeks in with my hair in scruffy plaits, I felt overwhelmingly underdressed for the occasion.

Nick was incredibly welcoming from the start, making a beeline for me to introduce himself when I arrived at the studio, clearly wanting to put me at ease. Eventually, a kind lady led me through to the open-plan waiting area where a group of reporters sat. I was given a cup of tea to drink while I waited. I sat quietly, listening to the reporters talk about assignments, equipment and what tomorrow might bring for them. I used the time to breathe slowly, evenly and deeply.

Nick entered the seated area and attempted to set up a TV screen in the waiting area so I could watch what was happening on the programme before my slot at the end of the schedule. When he couldn't get it working, he called over one of the team to help. When they were unable to fix it, another person was called. When there were four people gathered around the TV, all attempting to get it to work, Nick said, "You'd never think we all work for the BBC, we can't even get a TV up and working." I laughed. Everyone smiled and joked along. He was jovial, quick, but most of all kind, making me feel at ease as much as he could.

Somewhere near Stoke on Trent, I discovered the power of that news story. The sun was shining. It was a weekend, and people milled on and off the canal path. I was headed north. As I continued walking, one foot in front of the other in a steady rhythm, a little blonde boy of about eight cycled past as if his life depended on it. Just behind, a fair-haired lady followed on her own bike, with a little less wild enthusiasm. As she cycled past, she glanced at me and slammed on her breaks, screeching to a halt.

"Henry! Henry, stop! It's the lady from the TV!" The duo turned themselves around and headed back to me.

"Hi, lovely to meet you," I said, with a welcoming smile. "We saw you on TV, didn't we, Henry? We love what you're doing." Henry looked up at me blankly, blinking.

"Tell the lady what you have been doing since we saw her." Henry just kept looking up at me, wide eyed and silent. I smiled at him. Nothing. "Shall I tell her?" The woman offered. He looked at her and nodded. The resemblance, even without the same sandy coloured hair, was striking. "Henry has been making little treasure chests and gifting them to his friends. We've been getting lots of messages from parents who have said how happy it has made their children when they've come home from school." I got down to his level. "Wow, that sounds very kind. So, it's made your friends really happy, has it?" He nodded, just a little nod. "Wow," I said. "Do you know, because you made them happy with your kindness, they might now be kind to other people, and make them happy too?" Henry looked up, past me and into the sky. His eyes widened as though a penny was dropping for him, that he was realising for the first time that his actions had the power to influence others and he had chosen to use that power well.

We said goodbye and, as I continued on, I didn't question myself or ask myself why I was doing what I was doing for the rest of the day. I didn't wonder if it made a difference, this conversation starter on kindness. Today, no naysayer in the world could doubt me or question my sanity. Henry and I had given each other such great gifts. I felt sure of myself again.

The weather had been inconsistent but had certainly made up its mind by the time I headed into the Lake District. It was blowing a gale and the rain lashed down, whipping my face. I continued to walk down farm tracks and country roads as the sky got darker and the paths got muddier. I became resigned to it; I didn't wish to be home or in a different place. I just accepted this was where I was and what I had to do and, above all else, to keeping moving. Despite the wind pelting and swirling around me and the rain cutting into my skin, the rest of the day's walk was surprisingly easy.

By the time I made it to Windermere I had just a week left of walking. Windermere School was welcoming, and the students fully engaged in the workshops I led. The final activity was for children to design a presentation, in whichever way they liked, on the one thing they would change in the world and how. Their ideas were diverse, unique and moving, so much so that they brought tears to my eyes.

One idea that really stuck with me was a watch that monitored our behaviour. When we were good and kind, the watch would recognise this and give us points. Kindness was made into a competition, using addictive smart technology. Ingenious!

Setting off from Windermere, the sky was clear and bright, the air fresh and exciting. It was one of those perfect days for walking. I looked up at the hills ahead of me and felt no apprehension, just a sense that me and nature would get along just fine for a while. I was heading up over the Lake District hills. In around 20 miles, I would reach Pooley Bridge.

As ever, the natural world astounded me. It was impossible to take it all in as the browns and greens of the curved hills flooded my eyes. I climbed and climbed, losing the path every now and then and using Google Maps to re-right me. I weaved along the edges of the hills, knowing that I was so close to the end of the challenge. I only needed to worry about making the distance each day of that last week without causing myself too much physical pain.

My journey through the Lake District was the most stunning part of the entire walk. You would think there would be a well-trodden path I could follow, but no, I found myself striding up long grassy hills to get back on route and then walking back on myself when I took a wrong turn. On another day, in another mindset, it would have been frustrating. Today, though, I felt an inner calm. Whatever happened, I would make it to Pooley Bridge and then carry on to Gretna Green. I was driven by the people who were backing the challenge, those who had supported me and opened their homes to me because they believed kindness is not just important but imperative. With the power of the people behind me, I knew I could do it.

I arrived in Gretna Green and headed into the shopping centre to buy some chocolate before I set off by train back down south. I discovered that my debit card had expired while I was away and had no cash, so that was that.

As I wandered towards the train station, I felt nothing. I was neither elated nor proud. I had no desire to whoop from the treetops or tell anyone how I had arrived here. That was it. It was done. It had taken me five weeks to get here and it would take me eight hours to get back. No fanfare, just the knowledge that every person I met changed my life, and that a ripple of kindness had started that I'd never truly be able to measure.

# Chapter 17

## ElliptiGO World Record Challenge: 2020

### "Hello darling, you won't believe the weather!"

As I set off from West Markham, everything felt so fraught and I needed to get a plan together. I was glad to have some time off in Nottingham to regroup the next day. The wind blew fallen leaves in circles and a sense of unease swirled inside me too. Had I covered all of these miles just to fall at the last hurdle? I had been on the road for 96 days, completing 4,108 miles. With just 900 left to go, it was a matter of being so close yet so far.

In the UK, a new type of lockdown was due to begin. It was different to the lockdown back in March, when everyone had been expected to stay indoors. Now, we had a tier system with clearer dos and don'ts for each specific area. I had already had confirmation that the ride could continue, but I needed to consider what the best course of action was. It played on my mind as I kept cycling.

I was due to speak at The Kind Festival in eight days' time. After I chased them for some information, they sent me an email saying they no longer needed me. A wave of discomfort came over me. Time was never on my side. It would be unlikely that I would be able to organise another event to be part of on World Kindness Day, which was incidentally the day I would finish writing KINDNESS across England in Strava art.

"Hey love, how you getting on?" I listened to the familiar voice of my dear friend Sara, who called me to see how I was doing. "Um, not so good," I started. She listened to me as I shared all of the challenges I had to navigate, heard my tears and felt my anguish. When I had finished sharing, she took a considered pause and said, "So, what you going to do?"

She knew me well. It was exactly the right question to ask.

"I'll feel sad tonight, eat, watch something to distract myself, and then tomorrow is a new day."

I've known Sara many years. When we first met, I was a very different person to who I am now. Sara understood my younger self, stood by my side and loved me for who I was and for who I wanted to be. I had a desperate, impossible need to be liked by everyone I met and had suffered with poor mental health. Bad decisions often took control of me, but Sara saw through my pain and loved me all the same.

The need to be liked will plague us all at some point. Being liked makes us 'nice'. It means we'll avoid conflict at all costs, don't say no when maybe we should, and make sure everyone else comes first. Kindness is tougher. Kindness is about being authentic. It's about speaking up and addressing problems and most importantly honouring yourself. And, a lot of the time, it's about saying no in the right way.

The weather had been stormy and rainy with unforgiving headwinds. With just two weeks to go, the pressure was mounting. However, throughout it all, despite everything that went wrong, there was always time to laugh.

I called my mum.

"Oh, hello darling, how are you?" she said as she picked up.

"Yes, all ok, still pedalling, you know. What's been happening?"

I needed some normality, some familiar distraction. "Well, you wouldn't believe what the weather has been like," she said. There was a small pause while I considered my response.

"Do you know, mum, I think I just might."

With that we erupted into laughter. My mother is hilarious. It's not always intentional, but she's 'hold your stomach, bend over try not to pee yourself' funny.

There was no one about as I travelled the 50 miles from Marston to Rempstone. It was like the apocalypse had arrived and getting food was becoming a problem. Now I was linked to drawing KINDNESS as Strava Art, I was tied to pre-planned roads meaning I couldn't detour to find shops.

I called ahead to my next stop for the night, asking the owner if they could provide a meal or point me in the direction of a shop. "No, afraid not love, don't think you'll get much around here," she said.

As concerned as I was about my food intake, I was aware that there were those who had so much less. I was lucky and did not want to underestimate the power of my privilege. I thought of those who didn't just worry about finding a place to buy food but getting the money for it in the first place. How do we change the ever-widening divides within our society? I didn't know.

After another 10 miles of wondering what my next plan should be for food, I came to a small village with a pub providing takeaway meals. It was the stuff of dreams. I ordered two main meals and desserts to take with me.

Walking into the neat white room where I was staying that night, I pulled my food out of my bag. I felt the radiator. It was stony cold. The owner had told me it would come on soon. I could feel the chill in my bones. Needing to dry my wet clothes, I hung them on hangers in the hope it would warm up soon and crawled into the shower. As the warm water washed over me, I considered where I was. I had shelter and would do for the rest of the trip. I knew there were many who didn't have this luxury, so I counted my good fortune while I was able to see it.

I set off from Peterborough after a short interview with BBC Solent. I had just 650 miles left. I was now in a familiar setting and the roads felt like old friends. BBC Solent and BBC Spotlight have been loyal supporters of the message of kindness. So many media outlets want to focus on my grief and heartbreak, but I want to talk about how we need to act to make real positive changes. I still haven't got my 'radio pitch' right, but I'm getting there.

The roads were flat, and I was due to travel in one direction and then head back on the same road going the opposite way. It meant I would have the headwind one way and then the tailwind coming back. That was ok in my book.

As I came down the road to finish making the top of the penultimate 'S' in KINDNESS, road closure signs started to appear. I decided to carry on, as most of the time I was able to get me and Charis through. This time, I wasn't so lucky, and if you check out the S on the Strava Art, you can see it is actually a little short!

I turned back with the wind behind me and made it to a supermarket to restock on supplies before bed. As always, I went into the store to ask the manager if it was ok to park Charis at the back. They said it was. As I wheeled Charis through, a duty manager behind the counter turned to a colleague and said, "Bring your car in why don't you." It was not a joke; it was a snide and unpleasant comment. I put Charis at the back, and I faced him head on. He said nothing, no apology or explanation, just a general sense of outrage that I had called him out on his unkindness.

I experienced very little unkindness on the trip, but this moment stuck with me. It was a small interaction, but it is exactly what our society needs to remove. We need to call people out on their behaviours and educate them to be more emotionally intelligent.

I left Peterborough as the sun rose. The morning chill sliced into my bones, but nothing was stopping me now. The day's roads were pretty hairy, including an A-road which was like a motorway. I had just one day to finish writing KINDNESS, so I held onto that.

Toilets were increasingly more difficult to find, so when I eventually found some public toilets in Oundle it was similar to finding a pearl in an oyster shell.

I arrived at the hotel in Stanwick – my second-to-last stay of the challenge. A couple came out of the largely deserted building and the man introduced himself as the owner. "We don't live here normally, we live in Thailand, got stuck here in COVID. We are trying to get back as soon as possible. Maybe another month we hope." As the relentless drizzle fell upon us, I could understand why. We continued to chat about life and the hotel industry, and I managed to get some bike maintenance done. Every interaction fuelled my soul.

It was mid-November, and the day I would finish writing KINDNESS from Stanwick to Leicester. It was World Kindness Day. I'm not keen on the idea that we do something for just one day. Should we only appreciate our mothers on Mother's Day, or tell our partners we love them on Valentine's Day? No. So, while I loved the idea of World Kindness Day, I believed it could so easily promote surface-level acts of niceness instead of deep-rooted, continual kindness.

I had only 50 miles left to go and with the tracker set to cut off at 2pm. This would allow me to complete the last S and

189

then carry on to the final hotel in Leicester. I loaded up the bike and walked out the door as the rain began, heavy endless torrential downpour. I stopped and waited for five minutes, willing it to stop. The rain appeared to have eased so I went and got Charis out again. By the time I was outside it was pelting down again. I gave up and went back to my room. I waited until 10am. Time was not on my side, so I went for it. I put everything I had into those final few hours. Speeding along at times at 19mph, I felt empowered and free. When 2pm came I was in a flow and I didn't want to stop. I had completed the last S and only had 10 miles to go to get to the final hotel.

Originally, my route had incorporated an additional 500-mile circular route through Southern Ireland, but in the week before I was due to take the ferry to Belfast, COVID restrictions meant it was no longer possible. So, once I finished writing KINDNESS across England, I needed to make up the 500 miles that I'd lost. I did this by planning a giant heart shape on the flattest part of the UK, coming out of Leicester and spreading across through Norwich and London. After sharing this new addition to the route with Sunshine People supporters, they conspired to make their own heart-shaped routes on World Kindness Day. On that day, they walked, ran, cycled and swam in a shape of a heart wherever they were, tracked it and then shared the image. From this incredible show of solidarity, I know what it feels like to be truly humbled. The community had grown; I planted a tiny seed and then people spent time watering it.

But I wasn't finished yet. I set off in the dark from Leicester. It was a little like going on holiday, when you leave the house in the pre-dawn gloominess it feels like something exciting is going to happen. I've always had that reminiscent feeling, even if I was just leaving early for work.

The prospect of riding 63 miles ate into my mindset. I struggled on and at 20 miles in I stopped at a bus stop. I'd had enough. The route was no hillier than before, but the cold and drizzle made it feel like it was. I was starting to think maybe I could give up and finish now, maybe I'd done enough, inspired enough people. Every time I considered finishing early, the thought of the people who supported Sunshine People reminded me this was bigger than my aches and pains. I thought of all the talks I hoped to give to young people to inspire them to live their dreams and never give up. I had to live my own truth. Stopping was not an option.

So, I called Scott again. He listened to my woes, my quandary that I had no energy left, and the struggle to keep going. "You have two choices," he said. "You stay there and do nothing which will get you nowhere. Or you take a small tiny action that will get you somewhere."

With that I was heading back up the hill. Scott chatted with me for another hour and the next 10 miles disappeared just like that. Distraction was proving a great tool to cope with any scenario.

I arrived at the hotel busting for the toilet – I have never needed the toilet more than I did right then. Because of COVID and my slightly early arrival there was no one there. I hopped about for 10 minutes until they arrived and let me into to my room. There was no hot water and the room was chilly. They gave me a heater and I went to bed for a power nap while waiting for the water to heat up. My body was exhausted. When I woke later that evening, I was informed that Charis, currently parked in a storeroom, had a flat tyre. I went about changing the inner tube. It was the first time I'd had to do it, which was not too bad considering.

The next day when I woke up in Spalding, I couldn't remember where I was. I had stayed in so many places they were all merging into one. I got up at 5.30am with a pounding headache. There was a 20mph headwind forecast and I just thought, "Nope, not today, I am not pushing myself out that door."

Bed was calling me back. I pulled back the covers and climbed in. I slept fitfully, my body in desperate need of more rest. When I woke again it was 11.15am. When I opened the curtains, the sun blinded me. I was overcome by a feeling of guilt, annoyance and failure. I could have done it today. I booked another night at the hotel. I could feel the pounding, a dull ache, in each temple. My stomach was aching from hunger. I pushed myself to walk to a local supermarket and as I did, I found the strong headwind coming my way. The trees blew fitfully and, thankfully, I started to feel the headache lift.

An inner voice had been eating away at me, telling me I should do better and that I was failing miserably. The headwind, though, was saying, "It's ok, I would have held you back." I took deep breaths as I walked along, the wind and sun on my face. By the time I walked back into the hotel the inner voice was silent.

The next day it was dark and early when I woke, but I faffed and found excuses not to leave because I didn't want to. The wind was blowing, and I was not in the mood to complete the 55 miles to Cambridge. I'd done 4,600 miles and now, when I was so close to the end, each day was a serious mental struggle. Before, I'd been able to treat it as though it was a job. Now I felt like I'd resigned from the job but still had to work out my notice period. It sucked.

I knew from experience that I could change my mindset by repeating mantras and using simple counting techniques. When under pressure, your body wants you to stop, so it will preoccupy you with lots of negative thoughts, wanting and willing you to shut down. It takes all you have to keep your mind on the prize.

My mind kept wandering to limiting beliefs. Why were they still there? I attempted to concentrate on something more joyful, only to find the negative thoughts creeping back in again. In the end positivity prevailed. Training my brain had been as tough a workout as the mileage I'd covered.

I came to realise that the hurry was over. I didn't need to rush, I just needed to clock up the miles and get the World Record in the bag. Off I went, my nose filled with the wind and the driving rain almost drowning me. I'd not fixed the inner tube properly and the tyre continued to flatten. I kept pumping it up and couldn't understand what I had done wrong.

I called a bike shop 12 miles further up the road. They even offered to pick me up, but I knew it would be easier to keep pedalling and pumping as I went. Charis was a hefty piece of kit and I would only need to return to the same point.

Eventually, I reached the shop, drenched to the skin. "Ah, this is what the problem is," said the mechanic as he lifted a small piece of metal from the tyre with a pair of plyers. He examined the metal between the prongs. "Looks like it might have been the problem with the first puncture."

"Ah yeah, I didn't check," I said, wincing slightly. Even after all these miles, I still felt like a complete novice!

With Charis fixed, I peddled onwards. *'I'm Waiting for my Real Life to Begin'* came on my playlist. I sang along and was brought back to the romance and joy I felt the very first time I heard it in California, seven years before.

I arrived in California after giving up the house I had lived in with the ghost of Paul. My grandfather, another great love, had also died just three months prior. I needed the change, to escape from the grief. As I started my convertible car, the top mechanically folded down and I was bathed in the bright San Diego sunshine. I put my sunglasses on. The blue sea twinkled like a carpet of jewels. Arriving in Los Angeles, the coastline too tempting to miss, I hired an electric bike and travelled the white sands and blue seas for miles. I was free.

By the time I made it to Santa Barbara I was rested and coming into my own. Driving up the coast, walking along beaches, and ordering drinks in seaside bars felt like the tonic I needed. It was during that week of total freedom that I first heard *'I'm Waiting for my Real Life to Begin'*. In hindsight, I had indeed been waiting.

Back at the hotel in England's bitingly cold winter, I sat in a single long room with a sloping roof. Unusual, but cosy. I was in Sudbury and, with three days left, I decided I should do a check of my mileage. I'd been adding it up as I went along. This time, as I did the math, fear washed over me. I was 60 miles short of making the target based on my projected route. How had I miscalculated such an important number? It was a huge blow.

That night I slept fitfully, waking almost hourly with a start. In those moments of wakefulness, I started to make a new plan. The days were already high mileage anyway as I'd taken an unplanned day off back in Spalding. I looked over the map. The only thing I could really do was add the 60 miles to my final day, creating a 100-mile pilgrimage to the final destination of Leicester. In truth, I wasn't even sure I could do it. My body was already shutting down and my mind had reached the finish point a few days ago. I went back to sleep, making the most of every minute of rest.

The next day I set off in the dark. Today, I would finally visit the last city, Cheltenham that I had missed on the way up. As the sun rose through the mist, I was reinvigorated. The country roads opened out to me and a small hamlet appeared.

As my eyes adjusted in the dim light, I saw two horses in the middle of the road, lose and a little uneasy. A little further head was a van, and a guy with a bucket of nothing in his hand a rope in the other. He looked like he hoped to lure them in to keep them safe. I knocked at a nearby house to see if the horses were theirs. In the end the police arrived to resolve the situation, so I headed off. Horses had been integral to the start of my entire journey, when the stranger on the beach plucked me out of the depths of my grief. Now, as I neared the end of my challenge, here they were again.

Arriving in London in the rain, I enjoyed the flatness of the city. Could I do 100 miles? I really wasn't sure. I started to plan the route and tried to keep elevations to a minimum. I spent my evening playing about with the map until I found the best option.

I contacted Andy who I knew from a Facebook group for ElliptiGO users focused on health and a sense of community. There was never any unpleasantness, only support and love, because instances of unkindness were immediately called out.

"I'll happily ride with you on your final day," Andy offered. "I'll come and do the final 50 miles and see you into Leicester." I happily accepted. As it would be dark, Andy's company would be a huge comfort. I also had some ElliptiGO issues I hoped he could shed some light on.

"My chain is really loose now, and I can't tighten it. I think I might need a replacement," I explained. Right away, the solution presented itself. "That's ok," replied Andy, "I've got a spare and can change it over when I get to you."

Walking out of the room at Northampton with my belongings in my arms, I felt overwhelmed. Every step I took down the long corridor was important. This daily routine of get up, get ready, get going had become my life. Everything followed a process; nothing was down to chance. When I packed or unpacked my kit I had to be as efficient as possible, but now that was over. I didn't need to do any of it. No need to get my head in the game, to self-motivate or self-soothe. It was all over. Almost.

I called mum. "I'm coming home mum, just today to do."

"Wonderful, darling. I hope you won't be bored when you come back," she said a little uneasily. "There is nothing more I am looking forward to than being home and in one place," I reassured her. "I'll see you tomorrow."

I met Andy on the backroads. He was with his car, carrying the tools needed to fix the chain. But for love nor money, the chain wasn't coming off. I could feel the invisible clock ticking. Somehow, Andy found a work-around and undid some nuts that meant the chain could be tightened. A suitable solution to get me through the last 50 miles.

Andy and I chattered like we'd known each other for years. He had great stories to share about his own adventures and life in general. I could feel the evening chill long before darkness fell. The mist from our breath swirled in the night air. Country roads and a cloudy evening meant the ElliptiGO lights were the only ones we would see until we reached the outskirts of Leicester. That last hour was the easiest part of the entire trip. I felt in many ways that I could keep going, riding on an elation that was far beyond my physical capabilities.

We reached Leicester at 8.20pm. I was overjoyed to have finished. It was just Andy and I and a couple of official witnesses at the end of this incredible, almost unbelievable journey. I had done it. Everyone who helped me along the way had done it, too.

All the routine things I'd done each night for weeks, almost on autopilot, I no longer needed to do. I didn't need to get to bed at a decent time, or double check and download the following day's route, or get everything ready for a quick start in the morning. It didn't matter. So, I gave myself the luxury of wasting some time doing not very much at all except considering ordering a takeaway.

At 2.30am that night I woke with a start, a niggling feeling that I had forgotten something. With an audible gasp, I realised I'd not saved my 100-mile day on my mileage counter. It was reading at 99.4 miles. I logged the distance: exactly 100 miles, as the crow flies. My relief was palpable.

I woke again at 5.45am. It was my usual wake up time and I wanted to get back into a routine. My body, though, was heavy, my eyes were puffy, and every part of my being was in a state of exhaustion.

I got a shower, letting the warm water wash over me whilst I thought of breakfast and all the while, a sense of weight rising from my shoulders. It was then that I realised that the lump that had taunted me, was now gone. It was as if it had been a solid, unrelenting reminder of the words that blew in the wind; that hinted that I was not good enough to get the challenge completed. Today, it had no justification to stay within me.

I drove home feeling heady but anchored in the moment. I stopped and took my time at a petrol station, wandering around the food shelves, thinking about treating myself to a sweet snack. My food consumption for the past four months had been focused on nutrition, balanced and considered and functional. Now there was a chance for pleasure with no thought of the impact it would have on my performance.

Rounding the corner onto my parents' street, I felt the euphoria of finally being able to let myself believe it was over. I'd finished. My father stood in the doorway with his back to me, with my mum facing him a little further inside the house. My mother is a stoic woman, a 'let's just get on with it' type of person. However, in that moment, her face lit up and she came to hug me. It was my father who spoke first, "So, you found your way home then," with a grin.

A few days after completing the challenge I had a long, seemingly endless dream. I dreamt that I was on the ElliptiGO again, completing the World Record. So many of my dreams are based on a lack of completion, a feeling of not being good enough. But this dream was different. This dream was one of success, of not giving up, of finding a solution to every problem that faced me along the way. What was even more poignant was that this dream was in fact the reality. Even when the going was tough, when I wanted to give up and when the challenges felt too much, people picked me up and kept me strong. I devote so much of my life to the simple, powerful message of kindness, but it's the sacrifices of others that drive the cycle of love and kindness that ultimately connects us all.

# Chapter 18

## The end...for now!

*18,577,000 steps*
*8,525 miles*
*250,000 acts of kindness*
*Too many cities, states, people and counties to mention.*

There are so many takeaway moments from the past 10 years, but perhaps my 2016 challenge holds one of my greatest, cycling down the wide gravel track alongside the old railway line from my hometown to the next large town some 10 miles away.

I'd done this cycle more times than I can remember, but this time I had the life of another in my hands. A foster child was staying with me temporarily, and we were making our own Sunshine People kindness challenge, cycling along on borrowed bikes.

It was a cool spring day, unremarkable except for the fact that it was the four-year anniversary of Paul's death. Spring always makes me think of hope, the new blossoms a reminder of our versatility and fragility. But even when our branches are stripped back to nothing, we can choose to grow and bloom again.

We made it up the hill and sat down on a bench, opening up my backpack to reveal the packed lunch I had bought for us. We ate, looked out on the beautiful view, and after a moment or two she asked, "Can we see what other acts of kindness people have done?"

I pulled my phone out and started to take a look at the Sunshine People social media pages, sharing some of the stories that had been posted under #sponsorkindness. She listened as I wondered what she thought of it all.

"Shall we carry on now?" I asked, once we'd finished our lunch. "Yep, let's go!" She swung her little leg over her bike and started to pedal, and I quickly jumped on to catch her up.

In 2014 I became an approved emergency foster carer. It was something I had wanted to do for many years, even before meeting Paul. He had supported my dream to foster, but I was just too busy to commit at the time. I was working every hour of the day and sometimes also the night. Work felt like the wrong purpose, although I wasn't exactly sure what the right purpose was. Seeking it in service to others felt like a good place to start.

While I valued the company of children, I never felt the urge to have my own. I had friends who desperately wanted to get pregnant and I just didn't have that longing. However, I knew there were so many children without proper care and support who I could open up my life to.

After Paul died and my work changed, I looked into foster care again. I was told that due to the close bereavement I would have to wait 12 months before applying. It was the right thing to do, and 12 months later I applied.

There is something about fostering that instils a guilt in you for not doing more, for not taking someone forever. Should I have said that? Did I do something wrong? How will my actions impact them in their later life? You have a parent's guilt, but heightened, because the child is already vulnerable, and you are hyper aware that what you say and do matters even more. It could compound the trauma that has already happened in their life.

In 2016 I wanted to do something to commemorate Paul's death and at the time I was fostering two children. I asked them, "Fancy doing a 20-mile cycle ride for kindness with me?" "Yeah, I will," said one enthusiastically.

At 10 years of age, this little girl had already experienced more confusion, upheaval and upset than most people will in their entire lives. Despite this, she understood that it was up to her how she dealt with these traumatic events, and that her reaction would shape the rest of her life to come. There are many adults that have not had the chance to learn this powerful life lesson. Prior to the road that grief took me on, I'm not sure I'd fully learnt it either. She was just like me as a child, a people-pleaser, and I saw myself strongly in her. She didn't feel as if she belonged, struggled with herself and kept it all inside. I could really relate, and every day I wanted to wrap her up and say, it gets better.

As we cycled, the views of Dorset and the green fields stretched out between the hedgerows. She seemed so happy to be on the bike, not needing distraction or encouragement, having the end destination as a focus.

"Any more acts of kindness been done yet?" She'd ask over the course of the day. I'd check and report back each time.

The lesson I saw her learn that day I will never forget. Her life had not been easy. She was a bright spark that other people had tried to extinguish, but that day she was able to see that she had the strength to make great things happen. She was powerful.

When we reached the neighbouring town, we bought some sweets and as we headed back, I said, "Long way to come for sweets, hey?" She gave me a big grin.

The next day I was broken, struggling and moaning about my aching legs, but she stoically carried on, getting on with what she needed to do. I built a new level of respect for the little girl who, to me, had demonstrated resilience and pushed on through the challenge. She had made a conscious choice to succeed in the face of adversity.

We are all standing on the edge of a cliff, waiting for something to happen that will propel us into the perfect life we have always dreamed of. But the truth is, we're already in it, right now in this moment. This is our time.

Life's purpose, I have discovered, is about service, and from purpose springs contentment. Fighting change, resisting pain and not embracing our dreams is a waste. Happiness is not a constant state. How could it ever be? We would never know happiness without sadness. The ebb and flow of our emotional state is as natural as the tides, and to fight it is like trying to stop the waves from rolling.

We can be fearful of a future we know nothing about. We find ourselves second guessing what will happen, and if it doesn't work out as we expect, fear steps in and paralyses us. But what if it does work out? Why not say, "I'm not sure about this, but let's do it anyway and see what happens." Failure then becomes an old friend. It helps us learn more about ourselves, much more than success ever could. Trying and failing and trying again is what builds resilience.

Paul's death, while devastating, was in the end a gift. My recovery from the depths of grief and overwhelming sadness was humbling and gave me a new, unique outlook on life. I understood what death looked like. I saw it close up and I decided I was not going to go quietly. I was going to live my life, really live it.

It helps me to know that Paul's life and all that unconditional love was not lost — it has simply been passed on to others. It turns out my life is not about me at all. All of those times I got caught up in my internal stories and inner angst had been pointless.

I have discovered we are all here for one reason: to inspire and support someone or something else to be greater than they ever thought possible. I constantly check in with what I am doing, and the message I want to give. What will be enough? What do I hope to achieve? How do I expect the world to change? How will I know if it's working? These are tough questions, and I realise it is impossible to measure the impact of the challenges.

The important thing, when all is said and done, is the moment you are in. Always take the time to stop and stare, whenever you can. I have learnt to appreciate every moment in every day. When I want to tell myself I'm too busy, I remember busy is a state we put ourselves in. I can choose not to be busy. I can choose to take time each day to find deep connection and joy. Over the past 10 years I have met people who have gone through extraordinary adversity, and yet they choose to tell a story of hope and love. We each decide whether to carry our life in a gold bag or a sack of cloth. Neither is wrong, just different.

I wonder what it would be like to have Paul back, and feel his unconditional love again. He saw who I was and loved me deeply, despite all my faults, which became more reasons for him to love me. Equally, I know that my life would look very different if he were still alive. There is a theory called the butterfly effect, chaos theory. It is the idea that the flap of the wings of a butterfly in the Amazon can cause a hurricane in Cuba some time later. I have thought about this idea often on my journey of adventure.

The seasonal change from summer to autumn might be the greatest gift nature can give us. As the world turns from one colour to another, it might be mistaken for some mythical force at work. If you haven't, please do find a place somewhere when the trees start to tell a different story and stare quietly at the colours. Take time to give the leaves the respect they deserve. Through all the pain and grief I have fought, this action truly did become my saviour.

Courage is not something I consider much in my day to day life. I don't think I need more of it, or that I have more than the average person. However, the people I meet think I do. This got me thinking, where does courage come from, and how did the kid with a lack of bravery suddenly get it?

Well, to tell the truth, I've let go of fear. I accept fear is there to protect us, but in the modern world it kicks in a bit earlier than required. I held tightly to too many material possessions and when I asked myself why, it came down to fear. Fear of emptiness, fear of worthlessness, fear of a lack of value. The five week, 500-mile walk with just a bag on my back taught me that my greatest fear should be of storing 'things', of putting 'things' before people and not being true to myself. Letting all that go has been incredibly freeing. As each of the possessions I sold left my storage container, I felt freer, freer to be myself and to live a life that had not been travelled before.

I hope it has been clear that while there have been naysayers along the way, it has always been myself I have had to battle hardest of all. You can choose to ignore or walk away from the people who suck through their teeth or laugh at your ideas, but your head and your thoughts are what really decide if you will live the life you want. Our brains are wired to stop us from doing so much, however if we are comforting and compassionate to ourselves, we really can achieve anything we want.

My journey to date, and I'm sure yours too, has been full of twists and turns, heartbreak and love. We cannot fully experience joy without the crushing pain that sits alongside it. Pain and joy are good friends, and when we accept this, we welcome all of life's excitement.

I learnt more in the 10 years since Paul died than in all my previous 30 years of life. I learnt that the acceptance of deep sadness can also bring the greatest joy. I no longer need to keep moving forwards in fear of what happens if I stay still. I can be quiet with my thoughts. I can, just about, lie on the living room floor staring at the ceiling and know, in time, I will get up and keep moving on.

I am not extraordinary, I am ordinary, but I decide to do extraordinary things. I challenge myself to start a conversation that was nowhere near as popular 10 years ago as it is today. I'm not sure if my work has helped this collective of people who desire a change in the way we interact and live. I suspect it is just a drop in the ocean. However, with each drop, imagine the true utopia we could all form.

I have found it helps to be curious and ask questions, not only of others but of ourselves. I try to do this often, talking to myself as if I were speaking to a friend. *I am not good enough* becomes *I am enough*. The words we say to ourselves really do matter, and no one needs to accept the place they find themselves in. Instead of saying "I can't" the question to ask is "How can I?" Find out where the negativity comes from, and challenge that with action.

The biggest question we should always ask ourselves is this: "If I was told I had a week to live, am I living the life I want to, and am I doing the things I dream of doing?" If the answer is no, find a way, plan it out and go become your greatest self.

The problem with time is you don't realise how fast it passes by. On each challenge time has felt like an illusion, something that helps track my progress but in actuality bears no relation to real life. Time is simply a measurement. How long should something take to grow? How long we should date before moving to the next stage of a relationship? How long a friend must know us before we can open up to them? How long you should train for something? I have found time to be limiting in my life journey, but despite this I have made such strong connections with people I have only interacted with for minutes. They felt it as much as I. It was powered by kindness and ended in love. That is all connection is, love in its purest form.

When we commit to giving without asking for something in return, we are ultimately protecting each other. We are replenishing our collective energy. We become greater than the sum of our individual parts. The majority of humans want to help someone in some way. They want to support the cycle of kindness and give wholeheartedly. The hardest part, I think, is actually accepting this kindness, and this starts from within.

My journey as possibly the worst adventurer of all-time overflows with love and kindness. It is love and kindness that keeps me moving forwards, because when we work to inspire others, we can change the world for the better and create a kinder world. In the words of my father, "To treat suffering is worthy, but to prevent suffering is divine."

# Acknowledgements

I wrote this book and if I am truly honest, the first draft was a terrible book. It was only because of the incredible editing, feedback and growth provided by Lindsay Duncan that this book became what it is. So, if you like it, it is her you have to thank.
Thank you to my beautiful friend Laura who came in and did the final precision edit so kindly and became the new eyes we needed.

Thank you to key sponsors, Lombard International, MJB Precision Engineering and Hilton Hotels. Along with the many other organisations that supported the adventures.

A huge thank you to all the people who were mentioned in the book and the thousands who weren't, it is too long to mention, it would make a book in itself. People who were strangers are now friends, none of these adventures would have been possible or completed without you. However, I will say, thank you Sunshine People, a true machine of kindness generated by a community of people that I would love to take credit for, but it's not me, it's all them.

This has been a labour of love and I hope it shines through in the pages. Please do share your feedback on any platform that you can.

This book was written for you, may you take it forth on your own journey.

# About the Author

Nahla Summers by day is a Leadership consultant for Cultural change in organisations, by night the founder of Sunshine People and on the weekends the most questionable Adventurer of all time.

She has been awarded a Point of Light award from the Prime Minister for 'transforming the concept of sponsorship'. You will know why if you have read the book, but if you are reading the back first then this was given after cycling 3000 miles across America, having not owned a bike in 20 years. Walking 500 miles from South to North England relying only on the kindness of strangers. In 2020 making a World Record by going 5007 miles on an ElliptiGO through every city in the UK, in the middle of a pandemic. Whilst also producing the biggest 'Strava art' in England by writing KINDNESS across it. She completes these challenges and asks people to show their support by doing an act of kindness for a stranger rather than sponsor money to a charity. As the founder of the CIC Sunshine People, every year she takes on a new challenge and every year she discovers something new about the power that kindness has on people.

She is an inspiring and established speaker that brings an audience along with her on the adventurers through some incredible story telling. Among many messages that she delivers, she shares how we can change the chatter in our minds to allow us to achieve anything we dream of. How resilience is built and when the world gives us lemons how we can in fact make lemonade. How the actions of one can change the world and therefore what we each do really does matter.

She is also the author of several books. She won an award for most inspirational book in 2017 with a 'stellar piece of writing by a very talented author' for her first book, 44 Rays of Sunshine. With her second book, A Culture of Kindness, it is a powerful theory of how we can bring kindness into the workplace and not only be happier overall but also improve employee wellbeing. Her theory removes stress and anxiety from workplaces, therefore allowing increased productivity and profitable. Looking to change the way people and businesses co-exist with her talk, book and podcast of the same name, she is affecting us all with positivity of how we can live and work for a more sustainable future.

Find out more about her on her website.
www.nahlasummers.com

www.acultureofkindness.co.uk or www.sunshinepeople.org.uk

Printed in Great Britain
by Amazon